Urban Regen

Steffen Lehmann

Urban Regeneration

A Manifesto for transforming UK Cities in the Age of Climate Change

Steffen Lehmann
College of Fine Arts
University of Nevada
Las Vegas, NV, USA

ISBN 978-3-030-04710-8   ISBN 978-3-030-04711-5   (eBook)
https://doi.org/10.1007/978-3-030-04711-5

Library of Congress Control Number: 2018966749

Photo by Cida de Aragon

This Palgrave Macmillan imprint is published by the registered company Springer Nature Switzerland AG
The registered company address is: Gewerbestrasse 11, 6330 Cham, Switzerland

"This 10-part manifesto is a good guide to those of us involved with urban regeneration and is anchored by an interesting variety of real examples taken from cities in the UK and other cities. The author rightly argues for a more integrated approach to planning, with architects playing a vital role in good place making rather than striving for the spectacular!"
—George Ferguson, former Mayor of the City of Bristol & former *RIBA President*

"How we shape the future of our cities reflects how we shape the future of our respective communities—whether they are our economic, environmental or social communities. This book takes the learning and experience to date and moves it to a new level of understanding, to provide vitally challenging and thought provoking guidance. It fills a much-needed gap and offers guidance on the complex process of how to transform and regenerate post-industrial cities in the UK."
—Dr Louise Brooke-Smith, *ARCADIS Birmingham & RICS Past Global President*

"This book provides nothing short of a new blueprint for urban regeneration that responds to the pressing issues of today. Visionary and practical, it identifies key strategies for cities to realise their economic, social and environmental potential and unlock new forms of living for the many not the few."
—Professor James Evans, *University of Manchester*

"This book is a manifesto and a primer. It is a declaration of hope and a practical guide, a manual that sets out techniques for accomplishing a brighter future for the greatest number, in cities that are accessible, carefully constructed, attractive, inclusive, stimulating and full of life. It is inspiring and profoundly useful."
—Professor David Turnbull, *The Cooper Union, New York*

"This excellent new book is a practical and useful guide for urban regeneration of the UK cities and cities in general. The book is comprehensive and offers a clear vision and an integrated approach to planning. The suggested strategies can enhance the environmental quality of the cities and promote their economic and social life."
—Professor Mat Santamouris, *UNSW Faculty of the Built Environment, Sydney*

"Steffen Lehmann does it again! Another tour de force book and a fine if not the best follow-up and companion to Richard Rogers 'Towards an Urban Renaissance'. Ten sensible and well-thought out strategies of good urban planning are not short of a long awaited nostrum for cities that have never been more challenged and vulnerable by natural and man-made forces and disasters, but at the same time ready and willing to make a real transition and change towards sustainable urban regeneration and resilient futures. Brilliant!"
—Professor Tigran Haas, *KTH Centre for Places, Stockholm*

"This book was written to fill a much-needed gap: it offers guidance on the complex process of how to transform and regenerate post-industrial cities in the UK, where attention is turning to the regional cities."
—Peter Murray, *Architecture Writer, London*

Other Books by Steffen Lehmann

Informality Now. Informal settlements through the lenses of sustainability (forthcoming)

Growing Compact: Urban form, density and sustainability

Sustainable Lina. Lina Bo Bardi's adaptive reuse projects

Low Carbon Cities: Transforming urban systems

Motivating Change: Sustainable design and behaviour in the built environment

Designing for Zero Waste: Consumption, technologies and the built environment

The Principles of Green Urbanism: Transforming the city for sustainability

Sustainable Architecture and Urban Development: Proceedings, Volume I to IV

Back to the City: Strategies for informal urban interventions

Temporary and Permanent: On public space

Flow: Projects review

Absolutely Public: Crossover between art and architecture

Brisbane Towers – Brisbane Bridges: Architecture for the city

Der Weg Brasiliens in die Moderne: Einordnung der modernen Architektur Brasiliens

Rethinking: Space, time, architecture: Ein Dialog zwischen Kunst und Architektur

Tower of Babel: Architecture for the 3rd millennium

Steffen Lehmann: breite x hoehe x tiefe

Huelle, Schwere, Licht: Lehmann-Riccius-Sterf

Arata Isozaki: The 3rd Generation Art Museum

Foreword 1: Integration and City Leadership

George Ferguson

Cities have played a huge role in the history of the world but never more than they do today, given that the majority of us now live, learn and work in them. In Europe we are extremely fortunate to have a wonderful heritage and variety of great historic cities with a growth rate that is relatively manageable, but are we managing them well? There is at long last recognition that directly accountable city leadership and greater local powers are necessary ingredients for success, with the Government's enthusiasm for city and metro mayors.

When I first arrived in Bristol as a fresh faced architectural student in the mid-sixties the city was still in recovery mode from a war that had finished some twenty years earlier. The then city leadership's defiant answer to the damage of the Blitz was, as was all too common, to plan a brave new city of urban highways and high buildings; an 'anywhere' city for a new age of universal car ownership. Fortunately more enlightened forces, in the form of citizen action, saved us from some of the worst excesses and Bristol, like most UK cities, thankfully retains its distinctive character.

However, the planning pressures on our cities have continued to grow and it only seems right that Steffen Lehmann has kicked off his thoughtful *Urban Manifesto* with 'Cultural Heritage and a Sense of Place'. For the last twenty years, Steffen has been teaching and researching how cities will be used in the future. His 10-part manifesto is a good guide to those of us involved with 'urban regeneration' and is anchored by an interesting variety of real examples taken from cities in the UK and other cities. He rightly argues for a more integrated approach to planning, with architects playing a vital role in good place making rather than striving for the spectacular!

So what is good place making? It is often talked about but too seldom achieved. Some of the answers lie in these pages with their emphasis on healthy resilient cities that are focused on the wellbeing of citizens. This means breaking down our monocultures, tackling inequality, avoiding car dependency and fighting urban sprawl. Yes we need 'densification' to create much needed affordable homes and places of work and learning, and to make the most of what we have, but we need to avoid repeating the mistakes of the past with simplistic calls for high-rise buildings in a desperate race for numbers. It is the political chasing of numbers and short-term thinking at the expense of quality of life that has done so much damage to some of our most cherished places.

When I scan this *Urban Manifesto* I do so with the 'child test'. Does this make for a child-friendly city? If it does, it makes for a city that is good for us all. I look at the cry for a strong public space network, for a safe, walkable and playable city.

We are asked if we can ban polluting cars by 2030. We need exactly that sort of political courage, rather than kicking the ball down the line. What's more, we urgently need to reduce the domination of our streets by vehicles if we are to make our cities safe and breathable and help combat the shocking life expectancy differentials that currently exist between our affluent and poorer, more polluted, areas. It is in cities where an emphasis on public health, both mental and physical, can reduce the pressure on our desperately stretched illness services. The positive economic spin-off in terms of health, and cost to the National Health Service (NHS), would be spectacular.

It is our children who will benefit most from 'Green Urbanism', from active transport to breathable air to a more stable climate. They will be the ones to reap the benefits of maintaining our Green Belts and reclaiming a healthy relationship between city and country and the re-building of a regional food culture.

Waterfront cities, which make up the majority of our cities, have a great challenge ahead in terms of resilience to climate change. Can we turn that challenge into a resilience dividend with, for instance, flood defences that create recreational opportunities? Can we reduce the vast surface area of grim tarmac by building over our supermarket car parks to house people under green and photovoltaic roofs? Can we capture, for public benefit, some of that massive lift in the value of land that a good planning permission or new public transport system can bring?

We'll all have different priorities for making good cities but undoubtedly we would all benefit from a greater emphasis on young and old citizens, and inter-generational mixed communities. However, we should never regard a manifesto as a rule book, but rather as a flexible guide to be applied in different ways in different circumstances—to encourage each town and city to inspire its citizens and visitors by reinforcing its special character.

Vive la Différence, et Vive le Manifeste Urbain!

Bristol, UK   George Ferguson

George Ferguson CBE is a British politician, entrepreneur and former architect. He is Past President of the RIBA (2003–2005) and was the first directly elected Mayor of the City of Bristol, UK (2012–2016). He secured Bristol's status as European Green Capital 2015, as a founder member of Rockefeller 100 Resilient Cities and as a UNESCO Learning City. He has recently been appointed Bristol's first International Ambassador. He was a founder of the Academy of Urbanism during his presidency of the Royal Institute of British Architects. See also: www.peopleandcities.com

Foreword 2: Embracing Urban Complexity

Malcolm Smith

Patrick Geddes transformed the way I thought about cities when I first heard his quote—"A city is more than a place in space, it is a journey in time". In this beautifully simple statement he captures an obvious but often overlooked fact. Cities are in a continual state of flux; if not, they are more than likely in decline. I believe this flux is the negotiation between physical, social, economic and political forces. Only by recognising the transactional nature of cities, together with their evolutionary nature, can we begin to successfully set their future direction. The fundamental challenge is to distil key priorities for cities, some particular to a place, others more general to wider contexts, around which evolution can be directed.

In an age of increasing contextualisation, looking back in through the history of a place reveals the priorities of people in the past, and thus the underlying character of a place. The challenge is to avoid 'disneyfication', ossifying environments, freezing them in time as artefacts in danger of losing relevance to the changing city. The increasingly enlightened position of our heritage custodians allows cites to repurpose much of their historic collateral, in doing so beginning to recapture a sense of authenticity of place that has been lost. The challenge is to be able to distinguish what is of value and to be retained, and what is not and should be changed.

The challenge is all the greater in the immersion of the immediacy. The cacophony of issues facing cities cannot all be equal, and prioritisation and focus are critical. It was interesting to see this in the work of the C40 (a network of megacities), where different cities identified key needs as a way of focusing and delivering change. This is seen in our city mayors, who drive a focused political agenda such as air quality or housing. It reminds us that cities have 'entry point' issues, around which change is catalysed. Sometimes these are planned in manifestos, but sometimes they are not, such as climate or security impacts. The character of a healthy city is its capacity to respond rapidly to change, particularly as cities become the core competitive scale of global interaction.

The 'journey in time' through understanding past and present, sets trajectories into the future, allowing propositions of how change may occur to be tested and planned. Accompanying this must be the rigor of research and horizon scanning, to be able to quickly pick up the changing environment. Increasingly change is coming at cities through rapid disruption to historic norms, such as transport or digital systems. Disruption is not new to cities, but the speed of implementation and therefore impact is like nothing before. Tracking these new convergences will reveal the shape and form of future cities.

Geddes also reminds us that the city is 'more than the place in space'; he could have been inferring that it is about human experience, to which the physical city is just a foil. In an experientially based city, there is no doubt that meaningful, dynamic, accessible, equitable are characteristics which people look for.

Juergen Bruns-Berentelg, CEO of HafenCity Hamburg GmbH, described urban development—city making—as follows:

> Urban development is so much more than mere building. 'City' cannot be built, but must rather be induced in a deliberately heightened complexity. To reduce this complexity and try to carry out urban development with nothing but constructional aestheticism and form is one of the prime failures of the modern and postmodern age, and always has been.

His challenge to be more than 'mere building' is at the heart of the city. The city is not just the collection of separate pieces; it is an orchestrated whole requiring direction and care. UK cities are re-finding this custodian in their mayors, long lost in the piecemeal approach to development of the last 40 years. But complexity is more than physical, it forms the deepest parts of our sociological makeup. Over many years Richard Sennett has been revealing this to us. His thoughts can be captured when he says (in *Why Complexity improves the Quality of City Life*, 2011):

The quality of life in a city is good when its inhabitants are capable of dealing with complexity. Conversely, the quality of life in cities is bad when its inhabitants are capable only of dealing with people like themselves … drawing no collective strength from its mixture of different people.

So we move forward to ask, how do we guide the cities of the UK into the future? My sense is that it requires us to think of cities in a slightly different way. Three ways of approaching the city in evolution could be:

Integrated. Systems, challenges, opportunities must be increasingly inter-connected with each other, whether financially, social, or politically.
Agile. Cities are one of the key currencies of global competition. As such, they must not only have a clear and articulate sense of self and identify, but more so, must be increasingly agile in response to change.
Stewarded. Cities must increasingly recognise that one of the core values of the city is the collective nature of operation. Cites are not just the aggregation of their parts, but are also places of shared living and meaning.

Arup is very pleased to be associated with this publication, as we are fundamentally committed to making better places for people to live, and cities are at the core of this endeavour.

Arup Urban Design   Malcolm Smith,
London, UK

Malcolm Smith MArch(Yale) ARAIA, is an architect and the founding design director of Arup Urban Design, London. He joined Arup after completing his Masters' degree in Architecture at Yale University, and working in Australia. Malcolm is leader of Integrated City Planning and Arup Fellow in Urban Design and Master Planning, where he is in charge of a wide range of urban design projects both in the United Kingdom and internationally that have sustainable place making at their core. He was appointed as an Arup Fellow in 2011. See also: www.arup.com

Preface: Shaping Future Cities and Places

Peter G. Murray

In his book *Building and Dwelling – Ethics for the City*, Richard Sennett differentiates between two meanings of the word 'city'—the first is a physical place, the second a mentality, compiled from perceptions, behaviours and beliefs. Sennett uses French to express the two definitions—*cité* is what happens in and around the *ville* which is most easily, but inadequately in Sennett's view, translated into English as 'built environment'.

In any discussion about regeneration the *cité* and the *ville* are inevitably inextricably linked, and both are moving targets. The idea that the *ville* is a fixed physical asset no longer holds good—our attitudes to place and community change with astonishing rapidity. The post-war planning policies of Abercrombie et al. in the UK led to a hollowing out of city centres; in the less regulated US the same thing happened with the flight to the suburbs, the deterioration of the inner city exacerbated by the insatiable and growing demands of the motor car. It did not take long for people like Jane Jacobs in New York and Brian Anson in London to realise something was amiss and to stir public resistance to planning regimes that preferenced infrastructure over communities. But the damage had already been done. City centres had been hollowed out. John Letts, former planning manager at the Greater London Authority, suggested that Abercrombie's Greater London Plan, which dispersed large numbers of Londoners to the new towns of the wider south east, led to 40 years of economic decline in the capital; a clear case of the *ville* being more important than the *cité*.

By the 1970s the Labour Government were having to focus on the eviscerated urban centres. Inner City Regeneration became the watchwords—large swathes of Liverpool, central Manchester and Newcastle, as well as London's Docklands, were crumbling physically and economically. The failure of post war policies was starkly brought into focus by riots in cities across the UK in 1981. Although these have been described as race related, they were equally caused by urban deprivation. Michael Heseltine, as Secretary of State for the Environment, set up Urban Development Corporations to target these areas. The effect of regeneration plans for the centre of Liverpool are evident to any visitor to the city nearly 40 years later.

Lord Richard Rogers was asked to chair the Urban Task Force by Deputy Prime Minister John Prescott following the Labour victory of 1997. He called for an 'urban renaissance' based on the redevelopment of brownfield sites in areas with good public transport provision. The core ideas were based on Rogers' book *The Compact City* and demanded improved transport links, protection of the Green Belt, a network of green and public spaces, retrofitting and intensification of London's 600 local neighbourhoods as well reclaiming high streets. It was the period when public private partnerships bloomed with ideas of creating "opportunities for lasting regeneration".

The principles of Rogers' urban renaissance have formed the backbone of planning in London for almost all of the last two decades. The new London Plan proposed by Mayor Sadiq Khan is founded on the concept of 'good growth by design' which requires planning that intensifies and maximises mixed use development while retaining the character of existing communities. Its transport planning is based on the idea of connected communities and healthy streets where health and quality of experience is at the heart of decision making. Regeneration plans are focused on improving high streets, squares and public spaces; supporting markets, protecting small businesses and increasing community participation. The Plan will focus on a zero carbon London, cleaner air, a circular economy and a greener infrastructure.

But policies have to be delivered, which is why the strategies set out in this manifesto are so important. While the Mayor of London's healthy streets policy is one of the most advanced on any large city plan, the motorists' lobby have succeeded in delaying the implementation of new cycling infrastructure; local residents are stopping plans to pedestrianise Oxford Street, London's major shopping destination and one of the most polluted thoroughfares in Europe.

This book was written to fill a much-needed gap: it offers guidance on the complex process of how to transform and regenerate post-industrial cities in the UK, where attention is turning to the regional cities.

This highly relevant book is written in the form of an urban manifesto that includes strategies of sustainable urbanism to regenerate inner-city brownfield sites and presents a compelling case for practicing architects (and students), town planners, urban designers, urban decision-makers, geographers and engineers to take an active role in developing urban strategies and adaptation solutions to ensure our cities are resilient, resource-efficient and sustainable in the face of intensifying global warming.

We need a common understanding of how we can create cities that are both sustainable as well as great places to live and work. Essential to that is getting the right balance between *cité* and *ville*. Or as the great urbanist Jan Gehl put it: "First life, then spaces, then buildings".

London, UK   Peter G. Murray

Peter G. Murray is a prominent British writer and commentator on architecture and the built environment. He is currently Chairman of New London Architecture and the London Society. He was editor of *Building Design* and then the *RIBA Journal*, before he launched Blueprint magazine in 1983 with Deyan Sudjic. In 2004, he launched the first London Architecture Biennale (now the London Festival of Architecture). Peter is a keen cyclist and campaigner for cycling issues and supporter of this *Urban Manifesto*. See also: www.newlondonarchitecture.org and www.petermurraylondon.com

Reference

Sennett, R. (2018). *Building and Dwelling: Ethics for the City*. New York: Allen Lane Publisher.

Acknowledgements

This book is the outcome of several years of work and commitment of many. Firstly, I would like to thank all the people who made this book possible. It is part of a larger effort and broader research project to provoke debate about our urban futures and to synthesise new knowledge for urban regeneration and sustainability.

The topic of 'sustainable urban regeneration' is of particular relevance to me, as it has been a key theme in my research and teaching, which I have conducted as professor of architecture since January 2003, as former UNESCO Chair for Sustainable Urban Development in the Asia-Pacific Region, and in my work as an architect and urban designer with my own practice since 1993. In my work as a teacher of urban design, regeneration and city transformation I have worked with over a thousand inspirational students of architecture in various schools around the world. I have always had a strong interest in teaching architecture at the urban scale, and in the deep research of sustainable principles of cities, since I first established my practice in Berlin in 1993. I have been fortunate to be able to work as a full professor at great schools of architecture on five continents, the USA, Europe, Australia, Latin America, and Asia/China.

My warmest thanks go to George Ferguson (Bristol), Malcolm Smith (London) and Peter Murray (London) for providing generous and personal forewords and a preface to this book. A special thank you goes to my Ph.D. students and post-doctoral research fellows for their hard work, it is always a pleasure working with you on the *grand challenges* our society is facing.

I would like to thank the various cities and funding agencies supporting my research in urban futures and low-carbon, high-performance architecture. I would also like to express my gratitude to my colleagues at the Portsmouth School of Architecture, especially to Alessandro Melis, Antonino Di Raimo, Martin Pearce and Walter Menteth for their ongoing support and good conversations on the complex topic of urban transformation. The deep discussions with George Ferguson, Malcolm Smith, Peter Head and Daniela Melandri were important for the direction of this publication.

I am indebted to Rachael Ballard (Head of Science and Society) and Joanna O'Neill at Palgrave Macmillan publishers in London, for their support, trust and for managing the production of this publication.

I am also grateful to Claire Coulter and Natalie Poole at my Cluster for Sustainable Cities in the UK, for keeping track of the project and the wonderful job they have done in managing and improving the design and content of this publication. You made this a better book. Thanks for the chocolate!

With a little help from my friends and fellow scholars—my thanks go to the following strategic thinkers, scholars and stakeholders for inspiration and critique (in alphabetical order): Heiko Achilles, Pal Ahluwalia, Christopher Alexander, Thomas Auer, Joo Hwa P. Bay, Eike Becker, Christian Bode, Peter Brandon, Michael Braungart, Keith Brewis, Louise Brooke-Smith, Juergen Bruns-Berentelg, Scott Cain, Javier Castanon, Robert Cervero, Edwin Chan, Karen Chapple, Andrew Collinge, Annette Condello, Edoardo Croci, Mario Cucinella, Mahesh Daas, Luca D'Acci, Klaus Daniels, Cida de Aragon, Cees de Bont, Axel Deuschle (†), Bauke de Vries, Antonino Di Raimo, Ralph Dlugosz, Jinfeng Du, Chrisna Du Plessis, Harry Edelman, Hisham Elkadi, Sura El-Maiyah, James Z. Evans, Alfredo Fernandez-Gonzalez, Terrence Fernando, Jan Gehl, Georg Gewers, Tigran Haas, Catherine Harper, Manfred Hegger (†), Peter Herrle, Richard Horden, Simi Hoque, Donald Houston, Alvin Huang, Kurt Hunker, Claus-Peter Hutter, Toshiaki Ichinose, Jasuhiro Imai, Aseem Inam, Christoph Ingenhoven, Arata Isozaki, Mike Jenks, Mitchell Joachim, Ahmed Z. Kahn, K.K. Philip Kang, Irma Karjalainen, George Katodrytis, Trevor Keeble, Greg Keefe, Stephen R. Kellert (†), Jon Kellett, Jeff Kenworthy, Shahed Khan, Barbara Klinghammer, Joerg Knieling, Branko Kolarevic, Ralph Krohmer, Norbert Lechner, Pekka Leviakangas, Bart Lootsma, Piotr Lorens, Winy Maas, Simon Marvin, Adrian McGregor, Peter Murray, Boonlay Ong, Daniel Ortega, Dominic Papa, Mita Patel, Emily Penn, Igor Peraza Curiel, Rodrigo Perez d' Arce, Philipp Prinz zu Hohenlohe-Langenburg, Victor Regnier, Luis Rico-Gutierrez, Saffa Riffat, David J. Sailor,

Matheos Santamouris, Saskia Sassen, Ehsan Sharifi, Charlotte Skene Caitling, Malcolm Smith, Tim Smith, Werner Sobek, Thomas Spiegelhalter, Donovan Storey, James Taplin, Shane Thompson, Jeremy Till, David Turnbull, Rafael Tuts, Alec Tzannes, Nancy J. Uscher, Ben van Berkel, Andy van den Dobbelsteen, Tom Verebes, Thomas Vonier, Geoffrey West, Stuart White, Mike Winestock, Nyuk-Hien Wong, Wei-Ning Xiang, Wanglin Yan and Atiq U. Zaman. —You are all incredible!

Thank you to the Academy of Urbanism (UK). As architectural practice keeps evolving, some leading practitioners have been role models for the successful integration of urban research into their projects, making it a key driver of their innovative outputs. I am grateful to the following architectural practices for their inspiration and for pushing the boundaries of practice-based research: Arup, Aecom, UNStudio, Perkins + Will, Foster + Partners, Grimshaw & Partners, Shigeru Ban and Renzo Piano Building Workshop (just to name a few of the pioneers). We can learn so much from you!

This book would not have been possible without the generosity of the University of Portsmouth and I would like to thank for the support. Many thanks go to photographer Cida de Aragon for support and supplying the intriguing images for 'Life in UK cities'. I would also like to thank all photographers, architects and city councils for making images and information available. Every effort has been made to trace the copyright holders, and I apologise for any unintentional omission, and would be pleased to insert the appropriate acknowledgements in any subsequent edition.

Finally, a special word of thanks to my dedicated colleagues on four different continents: at the University of Portsmouth (UK), the University of Nevada at Las Vegas (USA), the University of South Australia (Adelaide, Australia) and at Xi'an Jiaotong University (China) for their encouragement and collegiality. My warmest thanks go to all the colleagues who have taken the time to share their amazing stories, projects and experiences.

London and Las Vegas, December 2018   Steffen Lehmann

Contents

About the Author

Steffen Lehmann, Ph.D., AA Dipl, AIA, RIBA RAIA AoU, is a leading voice, author and researcher in the field of sustainable architecture and green urbanism. Born in Stuttgart, Germany (*1963), he has an international reputation as educator and has made substantial contributions to the multi-disciplinary research field, leading large research groups on sustainable cities. From 2016 to 2018, he was tenured full Professor of Sustainable Architecture and Founding Director of the interdisciplinary *Cluster for Sustainable Cities* at the University of Portsmouth (UK). The Cluster is a research group of over 40 active researchers from a wide range of disciplines. Since October 2018, he is a tenured full Professor of Architecture in the USA, where he is Director of the School of Architecture, University of Nevada at Las Vegas. He is a Visiting Professor at the University of Portsmouth, and at leading universities in China and India.

Steffen has more than 25 years of experience in sustainable urban development and in the 'applied humanities'. Prior to his appointments in the UK and the USA, he was a tenured Chair and full Professor for over 13 years in Australia (2002 to 2015), where he held a number of senior leadership positions, ranging from Head of the School of Built Environment, to Director of two flagship Research Centres on Sustainable Design at the University of South Australia; he held the Endowed Chair of Architectural Design at the University of Newcastle (NSW). During all this time he has had significant responsibility for creating and leading new urban research formations, for which he has generated a large publication and granting output and a continuous stream of successful research students.

Steffen has advised over a dozen of cities on sustainable urban development, including Berlin, Shanghai, Singapore, Sydney, Melbourne, Adelaide, Abu Dhabi, Ho-Chi-Minh City, Oslo, Helsinki, Brighton and Southend.

He is currently Principal Investigator (lead researcher) of the interdisciplinary research project *CRUNCH – the Food-Water-Energy Nexus* (2017–2020), with 20 partners in 6 countries. He supervises post-doctoral fellows and Ph.D. researchers and has led the strategic renewal of the research and teaching areas of a large school, led teams of 120 academics, established university-wide research centres, and successfully managed large international multi-stakeholder projects.

In the 1990s, with his own design practice, Steffen was actively involved in the architectural creation of the 'New Berlin', designing and building a large portfolio of public and private works, including buildings at Potsdamer Platz, the extension of the Ministry of German Foreign Affairs, and the *Quartier an der Museumsinsel*. He has been invited as Visiting Professor to the University of California at Berkeley, TU-Berlin, and National University of Singapore; a DAAD-Professor at the TU-Munich, and UNESCO Chair in Sustainable Urban Development in the Asia-Pacific. In 2018, he was a Distinguished Visiting Professor at the Xi'an Jiaotong University in China. He is a member of the Royal Institute of British Architects, the Institute of Australian Architects, and the Academy of Urbanism in the UK. He was invited as keynote speaker at over 100 important international conferences, and presented at more than 500 conferences and symposia in 40 countries.

Steffen is a prolific publisher and has published 19 authored and edited books, numerous book chapters, articles and papers (300+), 5 journal special issues, entries to encyclopaedias, and has co-authored parts of important UN reports. He is currently a member of the editorial boards of six academic journals.

Recent book publications: The fruits of Steffen's research are prodigious, including scholarly books, journal articles and conference papers, invited book chapters, online podcasts and contributions to significant industry and policy reports. His most recent books are:

'Motivating Change' (Routledge, 2014, with R. Corker); 'Low Carbon Cities. Transforming Urban Systems' (Routledge, 2015); 'Sustainable Lina. Adaptive Reuse Projects by Lina Bo Bardi' (Springer, 2016, with A. Condello); 'Growing Compact. Urban Form and Density' (Routledge, 2017, with J.H. Bay).

'Informality Now' (forthcoming: Routledge, 2019, with A. Di Raimo & A. Melis). He is Editor of a book series on Sustainable Design for Routledge (London/New York).

Since 2003 Steffen has supervised numerous Ph.D. students and postdoctoral research fellows as primary supervisor in the field of sustainable architecture, urbanism and design theory. He is mentoring early career researchers, providing them with opportunities within his research group and ongoing projects to stimulate their independent scientific inquiry.

His research interests are in the following intertwined areas:

* Resilient urbanisation for low carbon compact cities
* Green urbanism theory—scenarios for the City of the Future
* Resource-efficient construction and modular off-site manufacturing
* Urban culture and new programmes for age-friendly public space
* Sustainable architecture, high-performance buildings and technology integration
* History and theory of cities, urban renewal and cultural heritage

His writings focus on creative strategies that architects and cities can use to reduce the ecological impact and become more liveable and equitable places in the process. For more information, please visit: www.city-futures.org.uk and www.city-leadership.com.

List of Figures

List of Tables

Photo Series

Setting the Stage: Life in UK Cities

Photos by Cida de Aragon

1

Introduction: The Complex Process of City Regeneration

Presenting a Ten-Point Strategy for Urban Regeneration of UK Cities

Complex Urban Challenges

Currently, about 60 million people move into cities globally every year (UN data 2018). That is over one million more people arriving every week in cities somewhere in the world, each with an expectation of better access to jobs, better education for their children, better health care, better housing and a better quality of life (Ehrlich 1968; Lehmann 2015c; UN 2016).

Urbanisation is an unstoppable phenomenon, and as more and more people live in cities, it is the cities that have taken centre stage as key players in the future of human populations. City management, governance, urban mobility, liveability and density have all become key themes of focus for politicians and decision-makers to succeed in managing urbanisation, but in conditions of rapid urbanisation (especially with the dynamic exploding urbanism of Asian and African cities), controlled sustainable development and carefully considered urban regeneration has not always been achieved.

The situation of growing cities in the European Union is similar: Currently (data 2018) over 70 percent of Europe's population live in cities, expected to increase to over 80 percent by the middle of the century. This translates to 36 million new

© The Author(s) 2019
S. Lehmann, *Urban Regeneration*, https://doi.org/10.1007/978-3-030-04711-5_1

urban citizens, who will need housing, green space, employment and health care by 2050 (data: European Union Commission 2018).

The choice is not whether a city will grow, but *how well* it will grow.

Fuelled by population growth, most cities in the United Kingdom are also growing. There is currently a total population of 67 million people in the UK, and the urbanisation rate is around 83 percent (2018), which equals around 55 million urban dwellers. The UK's population is projected to increase by 3.6 million people over the next ten years. We are also getting older: More than a quarter of the UK's population will be over 65 within the next 50 years, according to official projections. The number of people over 65 will almost double to 21 million by 2066, as rising life expectancy drives the 'greying' population. The fastest increase will be among over 85s with the numbers trebling from 1.6 million in 2016 to 5.1 million people in 2066. According to a recent study published in *The Lancet Public Health* (Jagger et al. 2018), more than one million more people aged 65 and over will need round-the-clock care by 2035. This will be an increase of over a third.

This means that existing cities must now be regenerated and improved to better deal with their growth, health, the impacts of climate change, an ageing population and the desperate need for new homes. Even Milton Keynes, once dismissed as a 'soulless new town', is now one of the UK's fastest growing cities, projected to reach half a million residents by 2050 (up from 250,000 in 2018).

But can urbanisation in the UK ever be sustainable? What will the cities of the future look like as the urban population keeps rising? How should we guide this urban growth?

Cities in the United Kingdom are facing new complex and challenging conditions that require resilience and adaptation to the environmental impact of global warming and social change. It is time to regenerate and re-engineer our cities for the age of global warming (Bertaud and Malpezzi 2014). High-speed rail will have to be a cornerstone of any future development plans.

While only 1.4 percent of the UK's land mass is covered by buildings and roads (for England it is 2 percent), urbanisation is one of the defining processes of our contemporary times, and our understanding of it, whether in theory or in practice, has reached a turning point. This book is part of the project to embark on 'a large-scale reinvention of how we live together, grounded in inclusiveness and sustainability' (Elmqvist et al. 2018).

The future evolution of cities plays an important role in limiting global warming to 1.5 degrees Celsius. Supported by countless research, the poly-centric, compact and mixed-use city model has emerged as the most promising urban model. It is based on a different urban paradigm, where electricity and transport systems are rapidly decarbonised, with all electricity generated from renewable sources. In the city of tomorrow, we will find that districts have been densified through intelligent urban infill; and that autonomous (self-driving) electric cars and buses are supplemented by electric bikes, e-scooters and bicycles, transforming the use of public space: less space will be wasted on car parking and roads, enabling more usable open space for walking, cycling and for vegetation; and in the city of tomorrow all inner-city brownfield sites will be regenerated.

One obvious answer to the urban regeneration challenge lies in closer collaboration between city leaders, industry (architects, planners and developers), the community and universities to provide solutions for clean growth and sustainable urbanisation models. All over the UK, a paradigm shift in urban thinking is now happening, where brownfield and waterfront sites are becoming urban laboratories, highlighting the need for participatory planning, social inclusion and new ways of 're-greening' spaces to transform our neighbourhoods, streets and public spaces. Juan Clos suggests that we should 'use our streets and public spaces as drivers of urban prosperity' (Clos 2013).

Let's start with a definition of what *urban regeneration* is.

Urban regeneration, also called urban redevelopment, is an elastic term that has been widely used for urban renewal projects that transform a large part of a city or area of properties (e.g. privately or publicly owned neglected land) within a designated renewal area by developing and changing the use of the land (Bianchini and Parkinson 1993; Smyth 1994; Landry et al. 1996; Leary 2013). Frequently, the redevelopment of the area is controversial and the mix of future uses, amount of greenspace and types of social amenities is hotly debated. More recently, the focus has been on renovation and adaptive reuse of existing buildings combined with new apartment buildings at increased densities. Urban renewal projects emerged in the nineteenth century in the UK as social reform and a reaction to the increasingly cramped and unsanitary conditions of the urban poor; for instance, the early nineteenth century urban renewal projects by the Peabody Trust, or by

John Nash in London, during the 1850s (Mumford 1962; Evans and Jones 2008; Roberts et al. 2016).

As the selected cases at the end of this manifesto show, urban regeneration includes smart infill housing, new infrastructure and the transformation of historic buildings for workplaces, education and tourism, culture-led regeneration and place making. New buildings are skilfully weaved into the retained urban fabric. Cultural institutions are central to the regeneration of cities, frequently combining civic functions and services with leisure amenities.

In this regard, the notion of *urbanity* is also relevant. Urbanity refers to urban life and refinement. David Chipperfield and Simon Kretz explain (2018, p. 26) that "Urbanity is about the quality of everyday life in the city. It is about the engagement of its citizens in its making, about avoiding the alienation that can come from living in a large metropolis. Urbanity needs to be cultivated."

Dealing with Urban Change

In *Massive Change* (2004), Bruce Mau speculates on the impact of new inventions, technologies and social events that are affecting the human race worldwide. It is obvious that the changing forces in the contemporary built environment, affected by digitisation, new transportation and communication technologies, revolutionary materials, and changing energy and information systems have commenced to fundamentally transform our lives.

Urbanisation promises a better life with efficient services, convenient connections and stronger economies. It also carries the risk of unforeseeable consequences (UN 2015). In 1961, Jane Jacobs published *The Death and Life of Great American Cities*, one of the first—and strongest—critiques of contemporary large scale urban renewal.

Growing cities generate conflicts that need to be carefully negotiated and managed. For instance, when the economy booms and new jobs are created, housing demand increases, rents go up and new residents take over the neighbourhood to change it. Density increases, subdivided family homes become micro-housing and manufacturing (such as 3-D printing or maker-studios, supporting the entrepreneurial community) comes back into urban neighbourhoods, leading to disruption of the 'old ways'. From the perspective of the affected community, those who have been living there for a long time, this change is often not welcome and they try to keep everything as it was. However, cities always change and are in constant transition, whether we like it or not. Just think of the unstoppable impact from digitisation, *Industry 4.0*, the sharing economy and autonomous vehicles.

Urbanisation is a major driver of land use change and environmental decline. Urbanisation affects cities' resilience in complex ways. The increase in urban areas has been linked to the impact of profoundly altering the urban habitat and a shifting relationship between the natural and built environments. Despite all this, there is growing recognition of the need for daily contact with green spaces and nature in order to live healthy, happy, productive and meaningful lives. This book deals with the need to reconnect cities with nature (through nature-based solutions, such as urban forests, orchards or constructed wetlands) and leads to a ten-point strategy for urban regeneration (Beatley 2014).

Underlying all strategies for urban regeneration is health and wellbeing. In fact, all policies for cities should be about health. Health and wellbeing has to become the main policy driver for all urban regeneration projects.

English urbanism, the birthplace of *Arcadia* and the *Garden City* concept, has never placed the urban above the rural. Greenery and the countryside were always running through the heart of English cities (Melvin 2018). Since medieval times, the particular character of English towns has been shaped by their interface between countryside and town, and an emphasis on food supply. The attitude was often *anti-urban*. The early settlements brought civic, commercial and religious activities together, and for administrative efficiency they were given responsibility for the administration of their immediate hinterlands. Think of the great cities of Bath, Canterbury, Norwich, York or Winchester, these towns were traditionally penetrated by fields, orchards, meadows and fish ponds right alongside their largest and most significant building, the cathedral. The urban model of terraced houses and buildings of rural origin, set on agricultural street patterns, became a familiar combination, celebrated by the Victorians (Melvin 2018).

The compelling vision of a self-sufficient garden city published by Ebenezer Howard in 1898 (revised and reissued in 1902 under the title *Garden Cities of To-Morrow*), aimed to combine the advantages of both urban and rural living. The idealised image of rural living with secured food supply while benefiting from urban economises was a fixed element in the collective English psyche. Garden cities were planned communities of 32,000 people, and the first garden city, Letchworth (located 35 miles north of London) was founded in 1903, followed by Welwyn some years later (in 1920). Over 30 garden cities were eventually developed in the UK, all on municipally owned land to capture the social increment for public improvement, not private enrichment (see Fig. 1.9).

Howard's vision and the garden city movement proved to be enormously influential in city planning circles throughout the world. The re-housing crisis of the 1950s aligned with post-War optimism manifested in the *Welfare State* offered an opportunity for the architectural and planning profession to rebuild the 'old' overcrowded cities. It was an era of socially progressive politics and promised utopia expressed in the new towns.

The internationally influential urban planner Sir Patrick Abercrombie (1879–1957) established the principles for regional plans, which set out redevelopment according to the modernist ideal of zoning and de-densification of historic urban areas. Abercrombie's plans in the 1940s established greenbelts to protect the countryside from urbanisation, while allocating some areas for new towns (Peter Murray argues in the *Preface* to this book that the post-war planning policies of Abercrombie et al. led to a hollowing out of city centres. He suggests that Abercrombie's *Greater London Plan*, which dispersed large numbers of Londoners to the new towns of the wider south east and north, led to 40 years of economic decline in the capital).

Entire urban populations were relocated to new suburban developments, the new towns, allowing inner city areas to be reconstructed. The 1960s separation of different uses through zoning (separating motor transportation, commercial and industrial uses from living areas) was in line with the international movement in urban planning following the prevailing theories of CIAM, Le Corbusier and later Team X, with its British exponents Peter and Alison Smithson. Many of the public buildings and residential towers built during this period suffered from poor quality of construction and maintenance; coupled with the partial failure of the modernist planning ideals, this resulted in a somewhat negative popular perception of the planning and architecture of the era.

Harlow was the first new town inaugurated in 1947, a brave attempt to renew the garden city for the age of the Welfare State, renewing an interest in allotment gardens for food supply. Hemel Hempstead followed in 1949, Milton Keynes was founded in 1967, and Thamesmead in 1968. Looking back today, all of these new towns are from the lost period of social aspiration in housing, before Margaret Thatcher's government took over, and these towns are still growing and evolving today (Figs. 1.1, 1.2, 1.3, and 1.4).

Figs. 1.1 and 1.2   English cities frequently have areas with undulating streets and cul-de-sacs which recall rural settlement patterns. The concept of the rural scenery and the *Picturesque* gave the illusion of living in the countryside while enjoying the benefits of the city. Source: Photo supplied by the author. Great housing estates commonly developed around their garden squares, as described by Hermann Muthesius in 'Das Englische Haus' (1908) and by Steen Eiler Rasmussen in 'Experiencing Architecture' (1962). Source: Photo supplied by the author

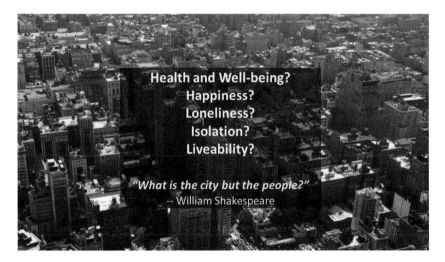

Fig. 1.3   The main goal of all city transformation must be to achieve and strengthen social inclusiveness to enable residents' health, happiness and wellbeing. Source: Photo supplied by the author

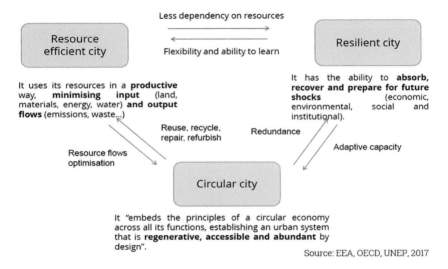

Relation between city concepts

Less dependency on resources

Resource efficient city

Flexibility and ability to learn

Resilient city

It uses its resources in a **productive** way, **minimising input** (land, materials, energy, water) **and output flows** (emissions, waste...)

It has the ability to **absorb, recover and prepare for future shocks** (economic, environmental, social and institutional).

Reuse, recycle, repair, refurbish

Redundance

Resource flows optimisation

Adaptive capacity

Circular city

It "embeds the principles of a circular economy across all its functions, establishing an urban system that is **regenerative, accessible and abundant** by design".

Source: EEA, OECD, UNEP, 2017

Fig. 1.4 There are different conceptions of future cities, including Resilient City, Resource-efficient City and Circular City. Source: OECD online

Other Drivers of City-Making

Cities exist because dense populations are more efficient at generating opportunities for trade, jobs and income. It has been proven that if businesses are geographically close to one another, people will flock there in search of employment, which will then lead to more businesses moving to these cities in order to be able to hire the best employees. This cyclical situation creates a common labour pool and can lead to more efficient trading and collaboration between companies. Cities exist because they create this kind of efficiency, which makes the creation of investment and wealth possible. The city of London is a good example for this, as too are regional growth hubs such as Manchester, Birmingham and Bristol. We often find that the richest countries in the world also have the highest percentage of their population living in cities (Florida 2002; Haas 2012).

Bringing people closer together has numerous benefits (Durkheim 1895), and developing existing brownfield sites is easier, as these are already well served by existing infrastructure. The *Charter of Athens* (1933) is an urban planning document published by the CIAM group including the Swiss architect Le Corbusier, which had significant influence and impact on modern urban planning theory in the second half of the twentieth century. Numerous architects blame the modernists' Charter as the reason why we still build cities that have too low density, with spaces predominantly for cars, and endure long commutes between home and work.

Suburbanisation, on the other hand, was a feasible urbanisation model in the 1950s, due to more widely accessible car mobility. We have allowed for our cities to be wrecked by the car, where the single driver per car (the majority in UK cities) represents the worst case scenario. But today, as the peripheries of our cities continue to grow and sprawl, it becomes obvious that mid- to high-density living is unavoidable, and new mobility concepts—including car sharing—are quickly growing (Cervero 2001). Some cities are ahead of others in regard to embracing electric mobility; for instance, 52 percent of new cars in Norway are already electric (2018).

Today, a number of critical transformations are fundamentally reshaping UK cities for the twenty-first century, including the impact of climate change, digitisation, information technologies, new employment and housing concepts, and the challenges of an ageing population—just to name a few—all necessitating new forms of infrastructure, housing and public space (Santamouris et al. 2001; Wheeler and Beatley 2004). The twentieth century automobile-dependent city has increasingly become unable to cope with the pressures and requirements of urban living and the need to curb global warming. Consequently, a new toolbox of spatial and infrastructural concepts and mobility strategies must be invented which will help to redefine the urban futures of our cities. At the same time, it is surprising that the shift in housing concepts has not yet had more impact on the conception of future cities: for instance, around 50 percent of households in Western cities are now single households, and no innovation yet reflects that over 20 percent of people in the EU are working from home.

What will the workplace of the future be, introducing new employment solutions? For instance, high-rise towers are rarely the best solution for work spaces; 5 to 7-storey office buildings are much more likely to improve communication within large company structures.

At the same time, the era of functional zoning and dispersed, mono-functional, car-dependant urban areas (e.g. sprawling suburbs on greenfields) is clearly over. Mixed-use compact neighbourhoods, reconnected with nature, and enhanced walkable open spaces form a new leading paradigm. In this, we recognise that each city has its own underlying unique structural logic. The performance and efficiency of a city depends on a range of criteria, but is largely influenced by its structural lay-out, urban form, degree of density, block sizes, and infrastructure and transportation systems. There are over 60,000 hectares of brownfield land in UK cities which already have strong transport links to trains and trams; these areas are the logical projects to tackle first and to regenerate.

Mixed usage is extremely important. Early regeneration schemes, such as London Docklands and *MediaCity* in Salford in the 1980s, made the mistake of just building offices, and are now seen as sterile and dead at weekends. The effect of mixed-use developments on the reduction in travel time and greenhouse gas emission can also be significant. Users of mixed-use complexes spend less travel time for shopping, entertainment and other activities, hence mixed-use developments affect activity-travel patterns and reduce emissions (recent research estimates that the travel time of residents in a mixed-use complex can be around 20 per cent less compared to residents living in suburbs or zoned, mono-functional developments). The more we can mix usage the better, as single use 'monoculture' development is always less sustainable.

Many cities are now creating inner-city hubs for light industry to stop manufacturing and other enterprises moving to the periphery or disappearing entirely, forced out by high rents or out-dated building codes. It is much better to keep workplaces close to where people live, connect communities and nurture creative growth (Figs. 1.5, 1.6, 1.7, and 1.8).

All cities are different, have different densities and vary in their experience, for instance their expertise and policies concerning the efficient use of land to prevent sprawl. Density is necessary for city life and vitality of public space, but we should be going for 'high density without going for high buildings' (this is further discussed in Chap. 3). At the same time, different concepts ranging from the 'Resilient City', to the 'Resource-efficient City', to the 'Circular City' have emerged. These interesting concepts are gaining more and more support in Europe and will be further explained in the following chapters of this book (see Fig. 1.4).

For 'city-regeneration', we need new buildings that provide a continuity of urban context, not objects in isolation. To create an interesting and diverse city, there should be programmes of changing intensities and varying densities of locally responsive designs. Here urban infill is of particular interest, because 'infill' architecture provides impetus for architects to develop unusual and innovative

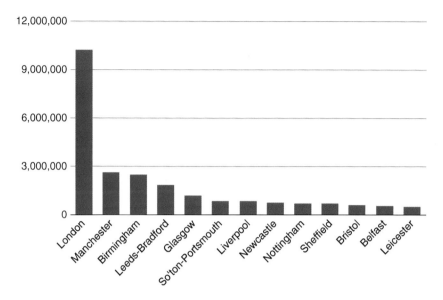

Fig. 1.5   Graph, size of UK cities, 2017. Manchester, Birmingham, Leeds and Glasgow are all significant urban centres. Source: Graph supplied by the author

Figs. 1.6 and 1.7   Community engagement events on the urban futures of our city, organised by the author in 2016–2017 to build long-term and meaningful collaboration for innovation. Source: Photos supplied by the author. Open dialogue and community engagement events. Architecture and urbanism is not just an individual pursuit, but a community undertaking. Source: Photos supplied by the author

design solutions. 'Infill' is an economical use of existing infrastructure and buildings that curbs urban sprawl, but must be used cautiously, as higher densities could draw in additional traffic, create issues of over-shading and decrease green space. For sprawling cities (such as we find in North American,

Fig. 1.8   The United Nations' 17 Sustainable Development Goals; Goal 11 is on Sustainable Cities and Communities (UN 2015). Source: UN online

for example), density will become a major issue: it will be crucial to reverse sprawl through smart rezoning guidelines for densification so better provision of public transport becomes feasible. The key question is: how could housing density in our cities be increased whilst at the same time providing better access to green space, and a greater mix of amenities and social space for existing communities? (Figs. 1.9 and 1.10)

Britain's Car Peak Was Around 2000

Like many other European nations, the United Kingdom has recently reached a maximum level for the number of private vehicles on the road. A recent study confirms the changes in young people's travel behaviour in Britain, and confirms that 'peak car' was probably reached between 1998 and 2000. Changes in living circumstances means that most young people no longer gain a driving licence or regularly drive a car. The number of teenagers aged between 17 to 20 years old holding a driving licence has plummeted by almost 40 percent in the last two decades (1998–2018; data by the Department for Transport). The number of young people in the UK with a driving licence peaked around 1994, but since then has been declining. At the same time, the level of cycling has remained broadly unchanged.

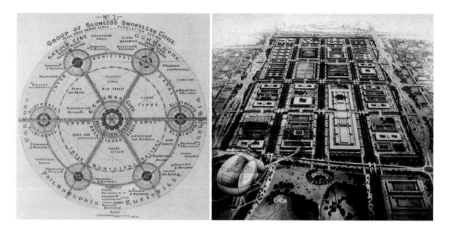

Figs. 1.9 and 1.10 Ebenezer Howard published the book 'To-morrow: a Peaceful Path to Real Reform' in 1898, which was reissued in 1902 as 'Garden Cities of To-Morrow'. His idealised garden city would house 32,000 people on a site of 2400 ha planned in a concentric pattern. Source: Open source image. The 1960s New Towns programme included the planned new town of Milton Keynes, a megastructure located halfway between Birmingham and London. Source: Open source image. Drawn by Helmut Jacoby. © Milton Keynes Development Corporation

There is much potential to increase the use of bicycles and e-bikes in UK cities. For short trips, these are the most efficient mode of transport. Cycling and walking provide enormous benefits to both public health and the environment. However, over the last decade, cycling trips in the UK have not grown. While the UK government is keen to encourage the use of active transport for short journeys, road infrastructure riddled with potholes makes cycling simply very risky. In terms of cycling and walking the UK has still a long way to go to match the best international models of Denmark and the Netherlands: Copenhagen and Amsterdam are also some of the safest cities for cycling because of their excellent cycling infrastructure and sustainable bike culture.

The rejection of car ownership by the younger generation is likely to become the new norm, as more people communicate online rather than face to face. A return to the level of individual car use in previous decades is unlikely, as many young people have become accustomed to a lifestyle in which private car use is less central than it has been for previous generations (Department of Transport, London 2018). However, there is no evidence that public transport, such as buses and trains, have managed to fill the gap in car usage, as there was only a small increase in the number of trips in the UK per person on public transport during that time period. This fact indicates the importance of young people having access to alternatives to the car for getting around easily, to access education, employment and social destinations. Therefore, we must now wholeheartedly invest in better public transport options, and support the use of e-bikes (electric-motor supported bicycles) and other new forms of low-carbon mobility, investing more in our city centres to create public space that is a joy to walk or cycle (CABE 2008). Around 50 percent of residents in Copenhagen and Amsterdam commute daily by bike. There is a strong cycling culture in Denmark and the Netherlands, and the UK has still a long way to go.

Although car mobility stands for freedom, independence and self-determination, it also plays an immense role in both city planning and our economic system.

There are a number of options to reduce car traffic. Tallinn, Estonia's capital city for instance, has made all public transport free for all. Stockholm and London have introduced a congestion charge for accessing the city centre by car, and Copenhagen and Amsterdam have drastically reduced the number of inner-city car parking spaces and increased parking fees. They have progressively reduced the amount of car parking spaces in the city centre by 3 percent every year—enough to make a difference over time and create more space for walking with wider pavements and cycling lanes. Numerous cities have introduced free-bike schemes which are popular for commuting the 'last mile' from the railway station to the shops, office or home. All these measures are effective as long as the quality and frequency of public transport is increased. Ideally, 90 percent of residents should live within a 400-metre walk to a bus stop and 800 metre to a train station.

This optimistic high-level guiding manifesto rightly argues that health, public space improvement and low-carbon mobility should be the starting point of all urban regeneration projects!

The long and proud history of UK cities is closely intertwined with the history of their railway lines. Today, high-speed rail systems are efficient and comfortable, travelling as fast as over 250 kilometres per hour. However, speed is not the only important factor. Railway stations in the UK and Europe are an integral part of the historic urban fabric, delivering their passengers right into the heart of cities and connect them to a range of other mobility options (acting as multimodal transit hubs). The regenerated railway stations will establish a civic destination that plays a fundamental role in the city's mobility system, while providing an active ground floor with a wide range of services, such as shopping, civic services or entertainment uses coupled with the transit services. This supportive mix of uses and the strategic adaptive reuse of historic structures will act as a catalyst for sustainable urban development that will positively contribute to local economic growth.

Around one third of all emissions in European and UK cities result from mobility activities, and we have not really managed to reduce this portion over the last twenty years. Improvements in the mobility sector are now urgently necessary. Incentives for behaviour change, car sharing and the reduction of car parking spaces will help to finally reduce emissions from transport. There are clever ways to facilitate changes in mobility: at HafenCity in Hamburg, for instance, value-capture from higher urban densities has paid for the extension of the city's subway system, boosting the use of public transport. The issue is, if you provide parking spaces you will have cars. There is evidence that if a person drives less than 10,000 km per year, car sharing is actually more efficient than private car ownership. If numerous European cities can all but remove the car from their historic centres, then we should be able to head along similar lines in UK cities. It will not be universally popular, as changing the car-driving habits of a lifetime can be hard, but it will be all but inevitable if the city centre is to become the walkable and popular jewel we want it to be. This is why urban regeneration must always have new concepts of low-carbon mobility from the beginning (not as a later 'add-on'). Autonomous, self-driving cars will not tackle the root of traffic congestion; however, getting people out of cars to use public transport, cycle and walk will reduce traffic congestion.

Architects ability to shape the city and engage with public attitudes has been eroded. At a point when we need most planning we have the least.—**David Chipperfield**

Can We Trust New Technology to Fix It?

Urban decline and the deterioration of parts of the city is often caused by lack of investment or maintenance of public space, and usually accompanied by a decline in population numbers and economic performance, low investor confidence in a particular area, poor quality housing, derelict land and boarded up shopfronts. The cycle of urban decline following deindustrialisation is well known and researched:

as deindustrialisation happens and industries and businesses start to reduce their workforce or relocate, it has often marked the beginning of urban decline with buildings sitting empty and residential properties becoming abandoned as areas' reputation declined.

There was a time in the 1960s and 70s when architects and planners believed in technological solutions to 'fix the problems of our cities'. These 'solutions' would often involve pedestrian access decks up in the air, connecting parts of large megastructures, rather than the more practical solution of walking on the ground. Milton Keynes and other modular new towns are often called 'megastructures' (see Fig. 1.10). The urban concept of 'megastructure' was first introduced by Reyner Banham in 1976 in his book *Megastructure: Urban Futures of the Recent Past* as an overarching term for the collective visions of building structures that shaped the 1960s architectural 'plug-in' culture (influenced by visionary urban thinkers, such as Cedric Price, Archigram, the Japanese Metabolists and Yona Friedman, Haus-Rucker Co, Superstudio, Archizoom and Justus Dahinden).

We need to consider the need for social good from technology. It would be naïve to rely solely on technological solutions to fix the challenge of poor urban quality, shabby public space, or the threat of urban decline. The time it takes for new technologies to be integrated is often forgotten, e.g. when we are enticed by new technology that has not yet been fully understood and accepted by the end-user. Autonomous (self-driving) vehicles are a good example for this. Autonomous cars are likely to have some significant impact on our cities, their car parking and public spaces, but nobody quite knows what exactly these consequences might be. Especially, what their unintended consequences will be. In fact, at time of writing (2018), no city in the world has any strategy today for how to deal with autonomous cars that are likely to be on our roads in less than five years.

There are different scenarios about the impact of autonomous vehicles, and their exact impact is still speculative. However, it is likely that as a consequence of self-driving cars, the streets can be narrower because we will not need as much space for parking or the separation of roadways, so the amount of public space is likely to be significantly greater. It is a new technology that has the capacity to dramatically change the way we use cities (Banham 1969; Callenbach 1975; Szokolay 2004).

There have been emerging technologies that have done this before—changing the way we think about urban living: the steam engine and railroads in the early 1800s enabled bringing a large number of people and goods into cities, hence enabling industrialisation; the supply of clean water and efficient sewerage system made living in larger cities more hygienic; the electric power supply and grid in the late 1800s allowed cities to grow vertically and made it easier to get around in subways and streetcars, and enabled modern communication; and in the mid-1900s, the introduction of the automobile radically transformed cities and concepts of urban planning, forcing us to confront the issue of space and traffic flow in an entirely different way. Most people think that the digital network revolution has an equally profound impact and offers tantalising possibilities for improving quality of life.

Some architects and decision makers believe in new technology as a 'magic bullet'. There is still a widespread belief that advances in technology 'will always save us', when in reality it can also take us further away from ourselves and further disconnect us from nature. Sure, technology makes our lives easier: navigation systems save us from having to read maps, and the microwave saves us from having to cook our own meals. We have more 'friends' online, yet so many of us feel lonelier and more isolated than ever before. It is worthwhile to remember that technology alone is meaningless until it is embedded into a societal context. In the worst case, too much focus on technology makes the city more vulnerable (e.g. to energy black-outs), more energy consuming and less resilient (Brown 2009).

Nevertheless, technology will be important to future cities and prices for new technical solutions (such as PV-cells) have come down. It is well documented that today, the largest portion of greenhouse-gas emissions from cities comes from their energy use in buildings (mainly for heating, cooling, warm water and lighting) and transportation. While technology on its own is not the answer to urban challenges, well-integrated technology can be an enabler for urban regeneration. If natural ventilation and daylight are maximised, it reduces the energy demand for air-conditioning systems and artificial lighting.

On the other hand, the benefits of technology can be immense, such as citizen-centric big data which has tremendous promise for better informing local planning decisions and enabling solutions for more responsive decision-making processes. Big data can make a difference for urban management and decision making, but we need to consider the social impact of new technologies. Technology alone will not fix the environmental crisis. The plan is to leverage new technologies: the purpose of digital tools and platforms is to act as enablers and catalysts for human flourishing.

Co-creating a Shared Urban Vision to Overcome Resistance to Change

From 2016 to 2018, my *Cluster for Sustainable Cities* coordinated a series of 'Urban Breakfasts', each attended by over 140 invited participants and decision-makers from industry, the community, local government and academia, with the aim of discussing and co-developing a better understanding of the drivers behind UK cities and urbanisation. The aim was to create a set of shared guiding principles, like an urban manifesto of sorts, for effective city transformation and to discuss how our city could best transform its neglected sites and post-industrial brownfields into a series of mixed-use and affordable housing quarters, which would help to alleviate the socio-economic divide between the city centre and the periphery. The university itself is a catalyst in urban regeneration of significant scale. This year-long process of discussion and visualisation of alternative scenarios was so beneficial that the idea emerged to make our thinking more broadly accessible to others. Subsequently, the reflective participatory process led to the development of this publication, with the aim of providing more general guidance on the urban transformation of UK cities (see Figs. 1.6 and 1.7).

During this co-creation process, the need was recognised to produce a useful shared statement of urban principles, a kind of urban manifesto of agreed guidelines, which focuses on the characteristics of a 'good place' and the strategies of sustainable urbanism. It was recognised that stimulating urban regeneration would depend upon an agreed and ambitious vision as a shared manifesto that attracts investment for future large-scale urban transformation.

Chapter 5 of this publication presents the outcome of this process, announcing the much-needed ten principles for first-class urban regeneration that have the potential (if approached simultaneously) to propel our cities into sustainable futures; an architecture of re-use that translates and combines the complex 'science of cities' and the art of urban and architectural design into actionable and practical guidance on how to regenerate cities.

Using public dialogue and debate to discuss visionary but grounded ideas for the UK's urban future, we explored the current transformation of UK cities from post-industrial places to knowledge-based cities that are more service and design-oriented. During such transformation processes, it is critical to explain to the population the reasons for urban change and to educate the public in good urban design criteria. High quality and successful urban transformation for the long term requires consensus and a clear commitment from the community, city leaders, planners and developers despite short-term thinking and political change. In this context, the media has an important role to play: communicating key messages for a sustainable future accurately via journalists is vital to avoid speculative comment, sensational reporting or confusion.

Cities are notoriously difficult to change. Recent urban regeneration projects have shown that the more modest and careful step-by-step incremental regeneration strategies are often the most promising and successful, with careful integration and adaptive reuse of existing structures—rather than large-scale vanity projects. The discussion also touched on the threat of gentrification: how can we ensure that the residents already living in the neighbourhood can stay there and that the rents will not become unaffordable for them? The resulting increase in land value leading to up-market developments often pose a threat to the social diversity of the city. The 'normal' city is where young and old, rich and poor, highly and less educated residents are living side by side (and not divided, as in some dated communities of reduced diversity).

Growing cities around the world struggle to maintain the character of their neighbourhoods and the socio-economic diversity of their people as housing prices, congestion and costs of living soar, and Manchester or Brighton are no exception. The case studies featured at the end of this book discuss the important issue of gentrification in more detail (Fig. 1.11).

Integrated Thinking: A 20-Year Strategy for Urban Regeneration and Regional Development of Our 2nd-Tier Cities

There are plenty of reasons why urbanisation and regeneration are seen today as the twenty-first century's most transformative trend. However, we must consider the limitations of urban design and technology, and be careful not to burden future generations with inefficient concepts or solutions that do not work or are not inclusive. The UN's *New Urban Agenda 2030* has set a high benchmark with its Sustainable Development Goals (the 17 SDGs, which were launched in 2015) for the type of urban development we should strive for, as well as a clear accountability framework for achieving it. The motto 'leave no one behind' is a challenge that should be applied to every district and neighbourhood.

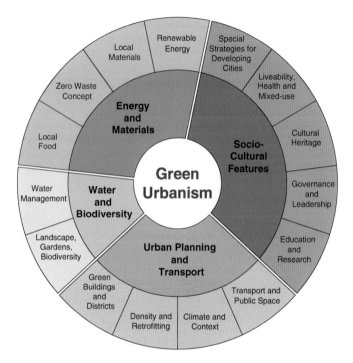

Fig. 1.11 The Green Urbanism Wheel developed by the author (Lehmann 2010). Source: Graph supplied by the author

The Sustainable Development Goals (SDGs; see Fig. 1.8) are a collection of 17 broad goals set by the United Nations; the goals are interrelated, though each has its own targets to achieve. Together the SDGs form the 2030 Agenda for Sustainable Development. SDG-11 is the goal for 'Sustainable Cities and Communities'.

The reader will realise that the manifesto presented here does not refer much to the capital city London; it rather focuses on the second-tier regional cities and smaller urban areas in the UK which are often overlooked. Interestingly, these cities and towns are in a better position to deliver faster on carbon reductions and regeneration goals than the mega-city London, because it is easier to guide smaller to medium-sized cities in new urban developments and to reshape their existing urban fabric.

In this, regional development is also a key theme, and there has been a discussion around the greater recognition of the UK's regional divide: this includes the geographic dimension to inequality and the difference in wealth between people living in the capital city of London, people living in the South, and people in the other regional areas such as the Northern cities.

The new high-speed rail line (HS2) project will improve transport links and see 330 miles of tracks linking London with Birmingham, Manchester and Leeds. HS2 is estimated to cost £45 billion, but when the necessary station upgrades are included it is more likely to be an investment over £90 billion. This is the most significant investment in the capacity and connectivity of the UK's transport networks for over a generation, and it is triggering the regeneration of cities along its route. Chapter 5 of this book includes selected regeneration cases of urban quarters and the construction of new neighbourhoods around future HS2 hubs, such as in Birmingham, Leeds and York.

The UK identifies 173 different regions, and according to a recent study by Ficco (2017), the UK is no more geographically unequal than other similar-sized European countries. The study shows that a similar proportion of the UK population lives in regions where income is typically below the national average as is the case in Germany or France (70 percent). The UK's policy commitment to equitable regional development, to create similarly equivalent living conditions in all areas of the country, has to be a driver for decisions of public capital investment, such as in improving transport links (e.g. the gigantic Highspeed-2 project), to attract business investment to the various geographic areas and away from the capital.

Anthony Giddens notes that we need to strengthen collaboration as well as political leadership. The UK Government can now show leadership in developing new urban regeneration standards to support best practice (for instance, by consensus-building through the visualisation of different urban scenarios, and by offering additional funding), it can finance more research in innovative regeneration methods, to implement urban living labs as demonstration projects, and underpin the collection of reliable data that will be needed to support better decision-making.

This kind of investment in urban regeneration will also support other promising initiatives that can lead to more sustainable cities. Some of the research we carry out in the *Cluster for Sustainable Cities* includes the study of the Food-Water-Energy Nexus, the Green Urbanism assessment framework for density, and the deployment of nature-based solutions to socially inclusive urban regeneration (as outlined in Chaps. 2, 3, and 4).

The urban future of UK cities requires us to work closely together and support local leadership to develop better strategies, policies, tools and projects that will help to address and resolve some of the core challenges of cities (including their complex relationship with their context, hinterland and countryside). Coastal towns such as Blackpool, Hull or Portsmouth, with their particular sea-level rise challenges, present unique issues to this future development.

Grounded in Inclusiveness: Brownfield Developments and Urban Regeneration

While UK cities have a significant history of housing, (just think of the immense housing programmes of the 1960s, the period of brave New Towns) there is now a massive need for new housing in the UK, especially in the affordable segment. New forms of urbanism always go hand in hand with new forms of housing—and vice-versa—and eventually, new forms and requirements of housing are likely to lead to a new conception of the city.

So one key question is: How can we best translate the primary legacy of the ambitious *Garden City* concepts and the brave *New Towns* programmes (from Letchworth to Milton Keynes) and their high aspirations into twenty-first century UK urbanism? Part of this is not to build on the greenbelts, but to maintain the existing urban footprints (through new tight growth boundaries) and to enable a series of interventions to carefully densify the already built up areas; including strategies for long-lasting change:

• Upgrading the neglected city centre, parks and public spaces,
• Including the adaptive reuse of obsolete urban infrastructure,
• Revitalising 'non-places' and enhancing the existing housing stock.

At the same time, the aim is to stop the decline of our inner-cities, deliver the millions of new homes urgently needed across the UK and develop existing cities in a way that makes them more resilient, liveable and sustainable. This process is about regenerating the existing spaces, not reinventing what 'the city' might be.

There is currently a demand-supply mismatch in housing: The greatest demand from UK's urban dwellers is for more inner-city affordable homes, but for a long time developers have built the wrong products, e.g. luxury apartments in high-rise towers or project homes in remote suburbs. UK cities need more affordable apartments priced at less than £500,000, most experts agree (the one-sided luxury development of Battersea Power Station area in London Vauxhall is an unfortunate example of providing a housing product for which there is no demand).

According to the Organisation for Economic Cooperation and Development (OECD), income inequality among adults has risen faster in Britain than in any other developed country since 1975, with wealth disparities in London and other large cities even more pronounced.

Most of the time, UK cities do not need spectacular change or large-scale vanity projects, but instead more modest and careful step-by-step regeneration strategies that get the best out of what we already have. This is not anti 'big buildings', but advocating a diversity of uses, scales and spaces that make for a diverse city (just like the diversity of today's society) and allow for urban experiments, e.g. experimenting with new forms of living and working, to open up the ground-floor of a building to diverse functions, or to create a footpath right through the middle of a block, as making the city more porous and better inter-connected will make walking easier and more interesting.

Brownfield development and urban regeneration are two distinct approaches—for example, brownfield development might refer to previously developed land that is not currently in use, whilst regeneration implies an attempt to reverse decline in the existing physical fabric of neighbourhoods or buildings. For both approaches, nature-based solutions can offer effective improvement of urban areas (as discussed in the following Chap. 2).

Some cities in the UK are leading in this development process and are ahead in their urban regeneration efforts, such as Bristol and Oxford, who have not hesitated to decide on and implement innovative strategies. The city of Oxford, for instance, was leading when it announced in 2017 that it will be the first British city to ban all polluting combustion-engine vehicles, which will be banned from entering the city's centre under plans to create Britain's first 'zero-emission zone'. Starting from 2020 only electric vehicles will be permitted on a steadily growing number of streets in Oxford. This will bring back a quiet urban environment with less air pollution that will enable natural cross-ventilation of buildings simply by opening their windows (something that is currently impossible due to the noise and air pollution).

To achieve all this and build local resilience through a wide range of community-based and environmental initiatives, our collaborative networks and partnerships are increasingly important. Enabling interconnected peer-to-peer learning networks with better information and knowledge exchange (as well as knowledge sharing between cities and other stakeholders) will facilitate more co-working between academia, communities and both the private and public sectors. The issue of urban sustainability is of such a multi- and trans-disciplinary nature that development of a meaningful research and innovation agenda must be a broad co-created effort representing all of society; it cannot be resolved by one discipline or group in isolation (Figs. 1.12, 1.13, 1.14, 1.15, and 1.16).

Figs. 1.12–1.15 Some of the best known examples of sustainable urban regeneration that have become global models of 'best practice': the green district Vauban in Freiburg (Germany). Source: Photos supplied by the author. Hammarby-Sjoestad in Stockholm (Sweden). Source: Photos supplied by the author. HafenCity in Hamburg (Germany). Source: Photos supplied by the author. Western Harbour in Malmo (Sweden). Source: Photos supplied by the author

Cities as centres of consumption

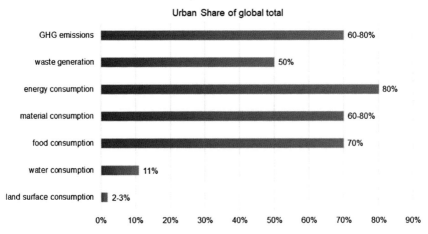

Fig. 1.16   Cities are hotspots of consumption and generating a large amount of waste. Source: Graph supplied by the author

New Types of Connectivity and Public Space Emerging

Cities mainly consist of housing and public space—these are their main ingredients. Urban regeneration started first with social programmes for housing and the creation of better public space. For instance, the urban renewal initiatives by John Nash in the 1830s in London were mainly based on slum clearance and social enhancements to improve health conditions, e.g. with the aim to bring back fresh air, sunlight and better housing to the overcrowded city.

Architects are slowly regaining their interest in urbanism and in thinking strategically about future neighbourhoods (meaning thinking beyond single buildings) and about what the city could look and feel like. Architects, planners, urban designers, geographers, social scientists and engineers have all got a crucial role to play in developing effective strategies and adaptation solutions to ensure our cities are resilient, resource-efficient and sustainable in the face of intensifying global warming.

Over the last twenty years, UK society has also become more diverse, complex and mobile. Accordingly, urban dwellers expect a better planned city with more housing choice. Society's changes in behaviour are evidently producing more sustainable consumption, waste management and transport (e.g. by changing travel behaviour or car-sharing clubs). At the same time, we find that more and more activities are being moved from the private realm into public space, ranging from family get-togethers to email communication and working. This means that we need to think about new age-friendly types of public spaces that allow for unexpected social interaction.

The most liveable cities in the world have public spaces that invite people to have a unique and diverse life experience. If we make the improvement of public space the main driver for urban design, we will promote social inclusion and get cities that are more interesting, safer and distinctively different from another. These public spaces can be modest and intimate in size, as Whyte and Madanipur have noted in their praise of small public spaces (Whyte 1980; Garreau 1992; Giddens 1999; Madanipur 2003). Just a few streets need to be turned into a pedestrian-only plaza to create a different urban scenario.

Buildings, places and neighbourhoods need to be flexible to work well over time. This means that they need to have lasting qualities, be resource-efficient, and make a positive contribution to their context and user-experience. Great potential for new public space is in the better use of rooftops for roof gardens and public terraces, repurposing omitted roofs as contemporary public spaces.

Urban regeneration goes hand in hand with new and improved transport links, as seen with the ambitious projects in Birmingham, Manchester, Leeds and York, where renewal is built around new rail connections thanks to the imminent arrival of the High Speed 2 railway line (HS2). The arrival of high-speed rail and vastly improved transport links into these cities means that adjacent neighbourhoods next to the stations will be transformed into new regenerated quarters. These projects go beyond railway infrastructure; they also enhance pedestrian connectivity, create new public spaces and parks, and a distinctive sense of place and genuine gateway that is integrated into the rest of the city. It is expected that these projects will reverse urban decline and instigate and support investment.

There is much innovative work happening that aims to redefine the streetscape, see for instance Alphabet's 'Sidewalk Labs' project: www.sidewalklabs.com. Their first living lab is the design of the streets for Toronto's new Eastern Waterfront development (one of North America's largest urban regeneration projects), where the latest in digital technology and real-time data will be used to create a more people-centred walkable neighbourhood around energy use, mobility options, retail and innovation (ideas range from bike-sharing to self-driving transit shuttles and so on). The aim is to create a streetscape that responds to citizens' ever-changing needs and explore a new integration between the road as a physical space and digital technologies (Sidewalk Labs 2018).

Over the last five years, nature-based solutions and urban resilience have become key concepts aimed at better understanding how existing urban scenarios can be transformed and enhanced to counteract environmental decline. The benefits of integrating nature in urban environments have long been recognised, both from the perspective of a changing climate and a transition towards healthier cities (Wilson 1984; Beatley 2014). The term 'Re-naturing' seems to suggest that new types of solutions are required that (in ambition, scale and innovation) go beyond the conventional benefits that urban green areas can yield. At the same time, new conceptualisations of urban models and infrastructure are emerging that can support new approaches to fuse the urban environment with nature in productive (environmental, social and economic) ways.

On the role of public space, Chilean architect Alejandro Aravena notes (2018):

> Public space allows us to transform the problem into the solution. This means: At the city level, allow public space (open urbanism) to perform as the cause (not the consequence) of development. At the building level, allow voids (porous architecture) to channel people's own building capacity and increase urban intensity.

Great Streets Make Great Cities!

A high quality of urban public space is ultimately the final purpose of architecture. Our role is to strengthen local differences so that public space is unique, not to homogenise the world.

Public spaces are the most precious common property that we have, they do not belong to companies or politicians but to all of us. Streets are crucial as they make up of 80 percent of all public space. UK cities have numerous great streets, just think of Gray Street in Newcastle-upon-Tyne, Mathew Street in Liverpool, Princes Street in Edinburgh or Marine Parade in Brighton. There are also less known and less formal streets that work extremely well, including North Laine in Brighton, Humber Street Fruit Market in Hull or Kirkgate in Leeds. Allan Jacobs has compared the world's best streets, and explored what the physical, designable characteristics are that make them great (Jacobs 1995). To answer the question, what makes a great street, he has surveyed street users and design professionals and has studied a wide array of street types and urban spaces around the world. Jacobs found that street connectivity and permeability have a major influence on the walkability of a city, but the link between social challenges and health and well-being in urban areas is still slightly unclear and needs to be better understood.

Much research is now on the way to clarify this area, provide evidence and fill the knowledge gap. The trend of public spaces becoming commercialised and privatised in UK cities is likely to be a dangerous one, consequently creating areas that poorer residents will be unable to enjoy.

The seismic change to retail in our commercial centres is enforced by 'big box' architecture at the fringe, and new online shopping habits that ignore the sense of place and shopping experience in a walkable town centre. Online shopping and large malls out of town have contributed to the rapid decline of the traditional High Street, and the future of retail is still unclear. In an era of growing privatisation of public space, cities are facing the significant challenge that investment in the public domain depends increasingly on the private sector. As a result of this re-framing of the 'collective agreement', the role of architecture has often been reduced to its shape and surface, rather than contributing to a new programmatic, civic or social dimension. There is surprisingly little innovation in retail, given that it plays such a significant role in our lives and has such a massive impact on our cities. The informal pop-up retail concept of *Boxpark* (for more background, see: www.boxpark.co.uk) has been one of the few new developments in retail: temporary use can activate places and combine street food with local brands, galleries and fashion shows.

The UK retail market has transformed over the last decade with out-of-city and inner-city developments and the emergence of e-commerce. The number of jobs in retail in UK city centres have been in decline, and this trend is expected to continue, with predictions of 900,000 fewer retail jobs by 2025 compared to 2014 (according to the British Retail Consortium there are a total of around 3mill. retail jobs in the UK, 2016). Added to this a renewed focus on city centres and 'new' spaces has led to a changing centre of gravity isolating peripheral secondary retail streets leading some areas to become disconnected and derelict. So what will the changing future role of the High Street be? Most likely, they will become centres of social activities and community-based attractions to deliver on a unique retail experience that internet shopping and large suburban shopping malls cannot provide.

As mentioned, gentrification has emerged as a serious threat to our communities. Many creative areas have become unaffordable: a victim of their own trendiness, they are now gentrified, contributing to rising real estate values in the area (just think of the Northern Quarter in Manchester, Stokes Croft in Bristol, or Brixton in London). Rising property prices not only force the creative people to relocate out of the area, but also push the poorest members of society out of their homes, adding to the housing crisis. *The Highline Park* development in the former Meatpacking District in New York City is often cited as an example of the destructive power of an overly successful regeneration plan that has not taken into account what the unintended consequences might be. These kind of projects need to include strong strategies for the delivery of affordable housing to retain the social diversity of the area.

The amount of affordable housing within a development is frequently a much disputed point. Ideally, all regeneration projects should include a significant level of affordable housing of 50 percent (including both shared ownership for first-time buyers and homes based on social rent levels for households on low incomes). Developers and councils can unlock the potential of underused sites by building more of the genuinely affordable homes citizens in UK cities so urgently need, and make a positive difference by ensuring developments include more genuinely affordable housing.

Internationally, there are a couple of celebrated regenerated neighbourhoods that have established best practice for urban renewal. Just to mention two in Germany and two in Sweden: the green districts Vauban in Freiburg (south Germany), the HafenCity port district in Hamburg, as well as Hammarby-Sjoestad south harbour area in Stockholm and the Western Harbour area in Malmo (both in Sweden) are prime examples of such programmatic innovation and socially-sensitive urban regeneration. Each of them provides good lessons for UK cities which have been emulated in the *Urban Manifesto*. These projects have new buildings contributing and giving something back to the streets and improving the overall condition, not as isolated or defensive objects ignoring the complex ecological, economical and physical conditions of urban space (see Figs. 1.12, 1.13, 1.14, and 1.15).

The *HafenCity* development in Hamburg offers a great diversity of new public spaces within an existing harbour structure that has changed from a sea port into a vibrant new city quarter, by regenerating and urbanising the shores of the river Elbe. This sustainable restructuring of an industrial wasteland is divided into 10 separate land parcels in a total area of 157,000 sqm, with an emphasis on integrating the existing historic heritage of the harbour into the new design development. Historically, the river Elbe was never controlled by locks; the annual floods are simply accepted, by integrating them as natural conditions from the outset. The flood protection strategy is to give water space to enter the basement (car parking level) rather than contain it, in order to protect the rest of the new district above. Two thirds of the new public spaces are floodable. It is simply accepted that these spaces will be flooded, and they have been designed with this in mind. The city lies at a higher level and is always protected from the water. Great care was dedicated to public space and a system of ramps, stairways and walkways connects the different levels of the promenade. All trees planted are at least 30 years old, which makes a significant difference in the perception of the new spaces.

HafenCity consists of ten different quarters, and over 13 billion Euro was invested between 2000 and 2019. A third (33 percent) of all housing in HafenCity is subsidised social, cooperative or public housing, added to Hamburg's affordable housing market in order to avoid gentrification and the creation of a 'gated community island'. The key parameters of HafenCity are:

- Total 157 hectare site
- 45,000 jobs
- 15,000 residents, with 7500 new homes (of this, 2500 affordable homes)
- 0.4 car parking spaces per residential unit
- 1 university with 5000 students
- 3 new schools and kindergartens
- 2 new subway stops within HafenCity

The HafenCity GmbH acts as 'entrepreneurial master developer' and is constantly looking for innovative ideas for how to develop and improve the quarter. For instance, value-capture from higher urban densities has paid for the extension of the city's subway system, boosting the use of public transport, and the underground car parking level is at the same time also the flood protection system of the district, allowing the flood prevention system to be privately financed (as the car parking spaces are sold with residential or office units). Since 2000, the CEO of HafenCity GmbH has been Mr Bruns-Berentelg; in private conversation with the author, he noted (2018) (Figs. 1.17, 1.18, 1.19, 1.20, 1.21, and 1.22):

> HafenCity was a steep learning curve how to best plan and implement such a large development. You don't do a plan and then implement it. It is much more complex and a constant learning process on feedback cycles to refine the development process. We act at three different spatial levels at the same time: at site, quarter and district levels. If one

car   bike   bus
Cities that are a joy to walk.
Too much public space is occupied by the car.
Use new mobility concepts as the starting point of urban regeneration

Fig. 1.17 Parked cars occupy and waste too much public space. This photo series shows how much public space is freed-up when 60 people arrive by bikes or bus instead of arriving in 60 cars (assuming the worst case: one person per car). Source: Photo supplied by the author

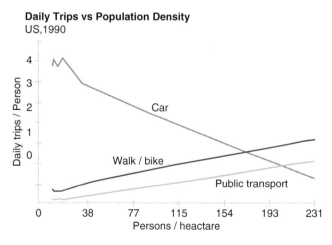

Fig. 1.18 Population density per hectare in relationship to mode of travel and daily trips. At some point, walking and cycling makes so much more sense than trying to get there by car! Source: Courtesy of Dunphy RT. and Fisher K

Figs. 1.19 and 1.20 Infill architecture where new construction is inserted on underused or vacant lots in already built-up urban areas within the city can be used to carefully increase density, often focuses on low rise, medium density and the reuse of obsolete or underutilized buildings and sites. Source: Photo courtesy of Peter Barber Architect and Morley von Sternberg. Photo 1.20 courtesy of Fletcher Priest Architects with BMD and PBA, London (Stefanie Turza)

Figs. 1.21 and 1.22 Public waterfront promenade, popular public space in Bexhill-on-Sea, East Sussex. Source: Photo supplied by the author. Public space along Chicago River. Upgrading waterfronts is a worldwide trend. Source: Photo supplied by the author

has a flexible framework of smaller site parcels sold to the private sector, one can establish an adaptive capacity to constantly adjust the masterplan to the new emerging realities.

If you provide parking spaces you will have cars.—Juergen Bruns-Berentelg

The governance-finance relationships in the urban regeneration process are also critical. New relationships are forming in 'Smart Cities,' which are likely to be leading to new types of workplaces and public spaces, as formal and informal gathering places are merging.

Another important issue is that much of our legal policy framework for cities is now out-dated. Traditional planning techniques that have defined much of the twentieth century seem to be unfit to guide the next step in the development of our cities. Most urban policies in the UK (and most other cities) are over 15 years old and were formulated in 'pre-climate change' eras, prior to impact awareness, and therefore are often ill informed. These policies need updating to encompass a new, integrated and evidence-based urban understanding. New policies will need to be introduced in order to better co-ordinate the adaptation of global warming impacts and housing needs, bringing people from different backgrounds closer together.

The best approach to the sustainable transformation of UK communities, and its enabling factors, are still unclear and for a long time have been an under-researched area. This knowledge will be required to reformulate the legislative framework, policies and building codes.

However, delivery mechanisms for transit-oriented developments (TODs) are still problematic and challenging. Only with the right urban policies (such as setback regulations, height limits and rules to activate ground floors) will we get better designed density, helping to maximise daylight and air flow. We can also reverse sprawl through smart rezoning guidelines and the better provision of public transport. In this, we must recognise the impact of new railway infrastructure on UK cities (for instance, the former railway area in York). One way to make public transportation more equitable and to promote equality is to offer it as an accessible, efficient and reasonable alternative to cars. Unfortunately, public transport in the UK is often too expensive for the young and the elderly.

Less Architecture, More Regenerated City: Why Urban Form Matters

A large number of scholars have researched urban form and its implications for city life (Lynch 1960, 1981; Alexander et al. 1977, 1987; Rowe and Koetter 1978; Hall 1988; Hall and Pfeiffer 2000; Koolhaas and Mau 1995; Jenks et al. 1996; Kostof 1999; Girardet 1999; Lehmann 2010; Cuthbert 2006; Head 2008; Gehl 2010; Glaeser 2011).

So much can be achieved by putting in place better urban form for more compact, walkable and mixed-use neighbourhoods! Rethinking urban form, green space and density will significantly help to achieve the greenhouse-gas reduction goals, as this is one of the key drivers for city transformation towards sustainability. Of course, it's not just a matter of solar collector technology, green roofs and electric vehicles; while all this is very important, it needs to go hand in hand with an optimised urban form and quality density. We know that walking, cycling and easy access to public transport and parks creates a healthier environment. This is also supported by a recent study (by Jagger et al., published in *The Lancet* 2016), which found that those living in city centres have a longer life expectancy than those living in the suburban or peripheral areas, because they are likely to walk more frequently over the course of their lives (the research was conducted on 6800 people from 14 cities in ten countries, with participants who were between 18 and 66 years old).

It is time to fully utilise the available urban design tools in the best possible way. Working at the front-line, many architects and urbanists have been pushing for the adoption of more integrated approaches, arguing that planning tools must be elevated as they are probably the strongest tools at our disposal to effectively and strategically regenerate our cities. Architects and urban designers play a critical role in developing alternatives to mainstream forms of urban regeneration. The tools at their disposal include integrated urban design, strategic land-use planning and smart zoning interventions, which are all important instruments offering multiple benefits to deliver a significant impact on the urban regeneration of a city, accelerating the transition to sustainable regeneration.

The way we conceptualise buildings and neighbourhoods has completely changed. Today, we are designing and constructing *high-performance buildings and neighbourhoods* that are so energy efficient (even producing an energy surplus) that their annual energy use can easily be offset with energy from renewable sources; these quarters optimise their operational efficiency with resilient and durable solutions which will stand the test of time. We design off-site manufactured modular homes which improve construction productivity, reduce waste and save time. We optimise operational efficiency with resilient, durable solutions that will stand the test of time.

Cities are more than just a handful isolated buildings (Lehmann 2015b), with different neighbourhoods and building clusters establishing a spatial relationship between each other. The best scale of intervention for urban regeneration is at the neighbourhood scale, by transforming the infrastructural systems. It implies that a group of buildings should be looked at as a 'unit' instead of single buildings. This scale of transformation can have a real impact that makes a difference. It will also offer opportunities to collect and analyse new data to better guide future decision-making on urban development (Girardet 2008) (Fig. 1.23).

The main function of the city is to convert power into form, energy into culture, dead matter into the living symbols of art, biological reproduction into social creativity.—**Lewis Mumford**

Fusing Different Schools of Thought: 20 Years on

Jane Jacobs (1916–2006) was a pioneer of urban regeneration thinking, and the theory underpinning careful transformation that respects what is already there (i.e. maintaining and reusing the existing urban fabric). For Jacobs, the key to urban rejuvenation was public space, and a good quality, walkable public realm, which is vital to everyday urban life as even small community gardens have the power to significantly improve quality of life for a large number of people (1961). A mix of uses means that people can live, work and play in the same area, with permeable

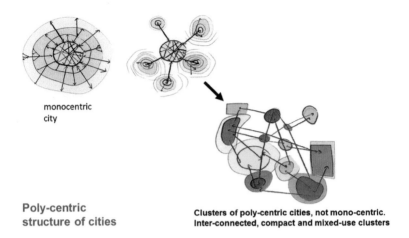

monocentric
city

Poly-centric
structure of cities

**Clusters of poly-centric cities, not mono-centric.
Inter-connected, compact and mixed-use clusters**

Fig. 1.23 As cities grow to over 500,000 inhabitants, it is important that they move from a mono-centric towards a poly-centric city model: an adaptive network of several centres within a compact, mixed-use and walkable urban form, where the sub-centres are inter-connected by efficient public transport (Lehmann 2010). Source: Graph by the author

streets and quiet manufacturing close-by. Numerous UK cities are now working hard to bring quiet, non-polluting production back into the city, including bicycle workshops, food production, artist studios, 3-D printing and other type of manufacturing workshops. It is about a 'city of short distances' where people do not need to commute long hours to get to their workplace or shop and home again.

Other urbanists and organisations have contributed key texts to the discussion of our urban futures and the limit of resources, including Meadows et al. (1972), Brundtland (1987), Register (1987), Von Weizaecker et al. (1997), McDonough and Braungart (1992, 2002), The World Bank (2010), Mostafavi and Doherty (2010), Urry (2011), UNEP (2011, 2013), and Lehmann (2010, 2015a).

The economic organisation of urban 'green growth' has been a subject of much research and debate over the last decade. There are many advantages to retaining a mixed economy with quiet manufacturing by offering affordable spaces within the city. Establishing mixed economies locally is much healthier and sustainable, for instance, by offering spaces for SMEs in areas such as furniture design and manufacture, or bicycle workshops, recycling hubs, software development, digital manufacturing and food production—just to name a few. Jackson and Papanek go a step further and ask if there could even be urban prosperity without growth, as the GDP-driven system of capitalism and globalisation destroys the ecosystem (Papanek 1984; Jackson 2009).

Recreating all sorts of affordable workspaces within the city is essential for maintaining or developing a successful mixed economy. This also includes artist studios and 'opportunity areas' as part of any mixed-use development, which provides the suitable and flexible sort of spaces. A lively start-up scene and affordable rents for studio spaces (like currently in Berlin, Lisbon or Prague) allows young entrepreneurs to save money and invest it into hiring great talent and building better products.

The city is, of course, always much more than just a series of individual buildings, gated communities or acts of architecture; it's about a combined effort to contribute to the continuous and holistic transformation of the urban fabric and its public spaces. The quality of public space has a direct positive impact on health and well-being, encouraging walking and physical activity, reducing obesity and potentially adding to life expectancy. Leyden has researched the social capital and health benefits from walkable neighbourhoods that reduce obesity and enable physical activity (Leyden 2003), as the public space network and green space integration have become main drivers of healthy and inclusive neighbourhoods.

Urban regeneration projects only work if they accommodate the complexity and diversity described so eloquently by Richard Sennett, Michael Sorkin and others.

Over the last years, I was able to observe the gradual gentrification of trendy neighbourhoods in the East London area of E1 around Brick Lane and Shoreditch. As real estate agents move in, this creative Bangladeshi quarter is following the fate of other gentrified areas before it—just think what has happened to Camden, Shoreditch, Hackney or Brixton over the last twenty years, where it has become increasingly hard to live a decent life on a low wage. Many low-paid service providers (think of hairdressers, taxi drivers, nurses, builders, cleaners and so on) need to live near their customers but find it increasingly difficult to do so.

The increase of city tourism has become another driver of gentrification. While a significant economic factor, mass tourism to cities has in some places become so excessive that it poses a new type of urban challenge: 'over tourism'. Travel is no longer a luxury good and the number of city tourists has grown so much that they end up destroying the places they love. Overrun European cities such as

Amsterdam, Barcelona or Venice receive millions of visitors every year and their infrastructure and public transport systems are buckling under the pressure. In addition, local residents begin to feel like foreigners in their own towns: in some places, locals have begun 'defending' themselves against the hordes of tourists who seem to be taking over, staying at short-term accommodation through Airbnb and driving up rents. For instance, in the Portuguese capital city Lisbon, the average rents have increased by 20 percent in only one year, in 2017. In the UK, relatively small but highly popular places such as Stonehenge, Bath, Oxford and Cambridge attract every year large numbers of tourists exceeding the number of their residents, and areas in these cities have become transformed into 'museums'. This development has been driving up rents and cost of living for residents, reinforcing the notion that tourists are invaders posing some kind of threat to the local population's cultural identity. In future, more sustainable forms of tourism that do not harm the cultural heritage and environment will become an increasing necessity for cities.

Inequality between regions in the UK and in Europe has declined between 1950 and 1980 as poorer areas industrialised and were able to catch up with larger cities. But since the 1990s, inequality is on the rise again (Schwarz 2000; URBED 2005). This has a dramatic impact on cities' population: highly skilled workers are moving to high-income places in the rejuvenated city centre (high-rise apartments near railway stations are especially in demand), while lower-skilled workers are leaving them. It means that with rising rents, poorer people who used to live in the inner city were forced to move to its edges (a process that Tony Travers calls 'the suburbanisation of poverty'), having to commute long distances from the fringes to their inner-city jobs (Travers et al. 2016). It is reversing the trend of the 1950s and 1960s, when many firms moved out of central London to new office buildings at the edge of the city or in the new towns built around its edges, creating a suburbanised workforce. Now technology firms like Google are leading the charge back to the urban core, as observed in Manchester and Birmingham.

For years, too little affordable housing has been built in the city centres, leading to more gentrification and commuter towns ringing the larger cities. Gentrification proves self-reinforcing, as new restaurants, bars and other businesses open to serve—and employ—gentrifiers. However, as Sarah O'Connor puts it: 'It is neither feasible nor fair to expect lower-paid workers to live in vast doughnuts around thriving cities, commuting ever-longer distances' (2018).

As a consequence of high demand and under-supply of housing, renting a home in UK cities can now take more than 30 percent of the salary. According to a recent survey by Adzuna on rental housing affordability (2018), the least affordable housing is in London (41 percent), Oxford (39 percent), Brighton (37 percent), Guildford (36 percent) and Milton Keynes (35 percent).

All experts agree today that urban regeneration can resolve a wide range of pressing issues simultaneously. Influential thinkers on urban regeneration—from Camillo Sitte, Ebenezer Howard, Geoffrey Jellicoe, Lewis Mumford, Kevin Lynch to Patrick Geddes, Colin Rowe, Jane Jacobs, Richard Sennett, Jeremy Rifkin, Christopher Alexander, Peter Hall, Richard Rogers, Jaime Lerner, Richard Florida and Jan Gehl—have all contributed their theories and thinking to guide our understanding of a 'good urban place'.

Twenty years ago, the *Urban Task Force* and Richard Rogers published the seminal manifesto for UK cities entitled 'Towards an Urban Renaissance' (UTF 1999) advocating the benefits of a compact and regenerated city. Many of the ideas from this time are still relevant today. Their text established a strong vision for cities in the UK founded on the principles of social well-being, environmental responsibility and design-excellence. Twenty years later, it is timely to reconnect and update these aspirations with this manifesto.

With the re-emergence of a regional development focus, attention has now turned to the competitiveness of the UK's regional cities; Manchester's current revival has a flourishing grassroots urban farming movement; Bradford has a growing arts and creative industry scene; Brighton is creating new places that bring socio-economic benefits; Hull has been the UK's *City of Culture*; and Bristol is experiencing an urban regeneration driven by innovative start-ups and a new creative-IT generation. The post-industrial regions of the north could do with a greater appreciation from London, a greater distribution of wealth and support from the centre.

The *Great Exhibition of the North*, based in Newcastle-upon-Tyne, was launched in 2018 and celebrates the story of the north of England through its innovators, artists, designers and businesses. Everywhere there is a race for talent, to attract the best human resources to each city, but these activities will all depend on affordable living costs and the availability of low cost space for studios—something that is the secret of Berlin's and Lisbon's recent success (and that London has lost a long time ago).

'Infill' means to replace and insert excellent buildings into small urban gap-sites—something that Hugh Pearman compared to *Urban Dentistry* and Jaime Lerner to *Urban Acupuncture.*

The careful densification of UK cities will become a driver for creating affordable spaces to live and work, just think of the many underutilised and under-used spaces in suburban back-gardens that do not justice to the high land values. For instance, there could be a lightweight kit-of-parts for prefab housing and studio additions inserted in gaps alongside existing properties or in back-gardens to provide additional independent and affordable living space or multi-generational adaptations. This would offer a flexible way to increase residential density and contribute to the housing crisis, while avoiding the possible negative side effects of densification.

In urban regeneration, it is important to address the real problems cities are facing, not just focussing on technology-driven solutions, but thinking of an inclusive policy framework and using transformative leadership to guide the process, with suitable indicators to monitor progress and implementation. Measuring consumption and monitoring resource flows is an essential part of our urban future, as noted by Rees and Wackernagel and the OECD (Rees and Wackernagel 1994; Alberti 1996; Talberth et al. 2006; Lehmann 2012; OECD 2012) (Figs. 1.24, 1.25, 1.26, and 1.27).

The city remains the best, but not the only, place to become fully developed as a human by today's understanding of what that means, and where tomorrow's understandings of what that will be are being forged.—**Peter Buchanan**

Figs. 1.24–1.27   The compact typology of the European city is an architecture of perimeter blocks. Six-storey block typologies in Amsterdam, Barcelona and Paris. There is a remarkable continuity in the urban pattern of cities in Western Europe. Source: Open source images, Academy of Urbanism (Stephen Gallagher)

Thinking Long-Term and Making the Most of What We Have

A thoughtful approach means to make more out of what is already there. An important principle is to trust in existing, readily available resources and structures, and to make the best out of them, instead of depending on external systems. Demolition and replacement of existing structures should only be considered as the last resort if adaptive reuse or renovation is not possible.

Adaptively re-using what is already there is a sustainable urban strategy that applies to the reuse of existing buildings, old infrastructure and public parklands. Renovation also contributes to historical awareness. The town of Hemel Hempstead, for instance, is a prime example of some of the best of Britain's first generation new towns that captures the spirit of the post-war era. Regeneration through urban improvement may come from different directions, in most circumstances it is about upgrading public space, housing, community services and transport, cultural and communal endeavours. In Hemel Hempstead, funding from the Heritage Lottery Fund made all the difference, as it allowed for the restoration of a linear public park with Geoffrey Jellicoe's *Water Garden* (which opened in 1960): tree planting, new pathways, foot bridges and seating areas were all part of the public space regeneration project. Prior to their regeneration, the Water Gardens were in a sad condition and the concrete bridges were crumbling. Now, the physical spine of paths and water as major linear circulation spine is again evident and, in addition, town centre improvements alongside the gardens include council offices and the open-air market space which has brought back outdoor urban life to the centre, regaining the confidence of the residents in their town's future. Urban regeneration is a much better way of managing urban growth than constant expansion of villages into small towns, of small towns into large towns and of large towns into conurbations (Lehmann 2018).

What is necessary are smarter public finance models to pay for urban regeneration without letting the banks get the upper hand of projects. In Sweden and Germany this is done by monetising the benefits: land value uplifts are effectively paying for new infrastructure and private developers make significant contributions towards social and environmental benefits from the project, and to build what the cities want. In return, they receive planning approval to develop the land.

Storyhouse cultural hub in Chester is a good example of how one prominent adaptive reuse project can become the catalyst for the regeneration of the entire city (see Fig. 1.29). Reopened in 2017, Storyhouse includes a theatre, cinema, library and restaurant. The project has unlocked £350 m of further investment in the wider city and it has reversed years of decline, transforming its formerly neglected surroundings and offering an alluring model for the integration of civic and cultural facilities. It is the first part of a larger masterplan to create a mixed-use district in Chester called Northgate. Bennetts Associates, the architects, commented on Storyhouse (2018) (Figs. 1.28, 1.29, 1.30, and 1.31):

> Housed partly in the renovated shell of a 1930s Odeon cinema in the centre of the city of Chester, and partly in a striking brick-and-glass new-build next to it, the project has created a new type of public building that is open 18 hours a day and reinvents the way a library is used and perceived. The complex includes a flexible main 800-seat theatre space with a fly tower, a studio theatre, a cinema and a city library. The new project is an inspiring example of championing and growing grassroots

Figs. 1.28 and 1.29   The repurposing and integration of former industrially used buildings is part of urban regeneration developments. Source: Photo courtesy of Peter Landers Photography (Herbal House). Photo courtesy of Bennetts Associates Architects (Storyhouse, Chester). Photos supplied by the author. Storyhouse Theatre in Chester is the adaptive reuse of a 1930s cinema complex (Bennetts Associates 2018). Source: Photo courtesy of Peter Landers Photography (Herbal House). Photo courtesy of Bennetts Associates Architects (Storyhouse, Chester). Photos supplied by the author

Figs. 1.30 and 1.31   More celebrated adaptive reuse, Anish Kapoor's studio. Source: Photo courtesy of Peter Landers Photography (Herbal House). Photo courtesy of Bennetts Associates Architects (Storyhouse, Chester). Photos supplied by the author. The Food Shed in Canterbury, a former train workshop shed. Source: Photo courtesy of Peter Landers Photography (Herbal House). Photo courtesy of Bennetts Associates Architects (Storyhouse, Chester). Photos supplied by the author

cultural organisations instead of importing them from elsewhere, something that has contributed to a feeling of local pride and to its long-term resilience and sustainability.

In Denmark, Germany and Austria, a couple of towns were able to reduce their annual energy bills and emissions by producing their own electricity with community-owned solar farms and anaerobic digesters. For instance, the Austrian town of Guessing introduced a system based on biomass, using wood waste from sustainable forestry practices as renewable energy to heat the town and generate energy. Twenty years ago, the town started to supply a local factory with free power; today, Guessing has attracted 50 new companies, which have created 1500 new jobs, and an annual revenue of $17 million due to renewable energy sales.

Less Energy Consumption, Creation of Waste and Use of Resources. Where Next for Urban Regeneration?

Urban regeneration always implies an improvement of the *status quo*. According to the Cambridge Dictionary 'progress' means "movement to an improved or more developed state, or to a forward position". Implied in the word 'progress' is the assumption that the current condition leaves something to be desired. On the other hand, the German word for progress is 'Fortschritt', which communicates a different message: 'Fort' means away, 'Schritt' means step, so literally translated 'Fortschritt' means 'to step away'. An interesting difference: the English word invites us to consider what we are stepping towards, while the German term has an emphasis on what it is that we are leaving behind. So it's worthwhile to reflect on the moment when we progress, what it that we are stepping away from, and what is it that we are leaving behind. Progress must always be a step forward.

Looking at the *Fortschritt* in operations at a larger urban scale and at urban systems (e.g. how a group of houses can potentially interact with each other by sharing supply and disposal systems) has numerous benefits compared to working at the scale of a single building. Today it is possible to integrate sufficiently mature, innovative technologies and implement these in low or mid-rise, high density demonstration projects in order to achieve a 'nearly zero-energy' operation and performance level. Using this approach, when

Figs. 1.32 and 1.33 'MediaCity Salford Quays' was an early urban regeneration project at a massive scale (2006–2013). This 80 ha mixed-use development on the banks of the Manchester Ship Canal in Salford and Trafford (Greater Manchester) is the home to key media organisations and anchor companies like the BBC, ITV, Ericsson, and the University of Salford, connected by a light-rail system. Source: Open source image. Link: https://en.wikipedia.org/wiki/MediaCityUK. West Court Jesus College in Cambridge, by Niall McLaughlin Architects (2018). Source: Photo courtesy of Niall McLaughlin Architects, London (Bryony Jones; photo: Peter Cook)

compared to business-as-usual, UK cities could deliver on the following ambitious and measurable benchmarks:

- 50% less car use
- 30% increase in use of public transport
- Min. 20% of all trips by bicycle or e-bikes
- 50% less energy use
- Over 30% energy from on-site renewables
- 50% less water use
- Over 75% waste recycling rate
- Access to at least 20sqm green space per capita

In the next five years we will see that further innovative solutions will become available and affordable for implementation and demonstration that will enable significant acceleration of their uptake. Once buildings require less energy and resources, the network capacity and infrastructural systems can be reduced in size; e.g. halving the building energy needs means that on-site photovoltaics make a larger contribution towards meeting demand (Figs. 1.32 and 1.33).

The ability to break the planning rules must be one of the top tools in our city-regenerating tool box.—George Ferguson

The Way Forward: An Interdisciplinary and Collaborative Research Agenda for Cities

The practice of architecture and urban design is always evolving due to new trends, changing needs, different conditions and circumstances that are to be met. However, today it is other disciplines that have more power to shape the built environment, e.g. Amazon and Google probably have more influence and impact on the creation of new public space typologies or mobility concepts than architects or urban designers. As a consequence, new questions are to be asked, and new research inquiries to be made, that keep our professions relevant. The main drive for research in the field of cities is that urban projects are becoming more complex and increasingly concerning issues of sustainability and urban ecology (Hill 2013; Hensel and Nilsson 2016).

Between practitioners a growing interest has emerged in the systemic inquiry of theoretical and practical knowledge across varied fields of disciplines. The need to rethink and regenerate our existing neighbourhoods (and to deal with their social complexity) is asking for an impactful research agenda that can guide the design efforts in meeting the new challenges. The future is less about new buildings on greenfields but rather about qualifying the already existing city and building stock. The aim is now to turn our research investigations into systemic approaches and methods of urban regeneration. This can only be useful, as architects and planners with expertise in this field will be able to secure and increase their influence (Lehmann 2015c, 2016).

Closer cooperation between citizens, civil society actors, companies and municipalities is necessary to solve societal challenges, given the urgency of understanding the options for an urbanising country. However, the numerous initiatives including co-creation workshops, urban living labs, smart city pilots and urban innovation initiatives have proven difficult to deliver and to move from short-term citizen involvement initiatives to a sustained practice where long-term citizen involvement is truly incorporated. The most promising way is to work on a specific city case where a pilot project is transformed in practice to demonstrate the benefits, to develop new tools and methods together, and to build interdisciplinary knowledge around a systems approach. This can be done by providing a synthesis of the evolving methods, knowledge and analysis necessary to enable the innovation required to regenerate cities. This manifesto aims to exactly do this.

To achieve sustainable urban regeneration, urbanists increasingly draw input and expertise from other disciplines to integrate directly into architectural and urban strategies, and to provide new directions in urban research that will help us achieve the regenerated cities we want now and in the future. Demand-forecasting and visualisation of alternative future scenarios has become a major instrument for successful community engagement. All major urban regeneration projects should be accompanied by research that provides reliable data for decision makers (Lehmann et al. 2013). Architecture has always been an active practice that operates as an agent of cultural transformation and interdisciplinary change. We must now ask: What are the research agendas and the most suitable forms of intellectual inquiry that can resolve urban challenges and facilitate working across traditional disciplinary boundaries to create a new *Science of Cities*?

City governments themselves are increasingly leaders in the transition to more sustainable and resilient pathways, but they still require support from business and academia. This is the reason why the *Cluster for Sustainable Cities* was established as an interdisciplinary research, design and engagement platform, focused on the rapidly changing conditions of urban futures. The Cluster's mission is to influence and transform the way we approach the design of future cities. With the aim of forecasting, influencing and shaping new models of urbanism, the Cluster is a university-wide initiative combining expertise throughout the University of Portsmouth, with over 40 members from its five faculties.

The Cluster is also an evolving platform for future policy and action focused on new forms of urban research. This includes engagement with urban leaders, decision- and policymakers who are fundamental to the Cluster's ability to have lasting local and global impact on the strategic re-conception of our cities. The complex conditions that comprise the city—social, environmental, economic, cultural, health, governance, and infrastructural—must be fully acknowledged.

Here, twenty years after the seminal text 'Towards an Urban Renaissance' (UTF 1999) was published, I present ten principle strategies for urban regeneration that I believe will make a positive difference, and reconnect to the seminal text published

Figs. 1.34 and 1.35 Working in the city: the mixed-use city reintegrates production and mixes living with working, retail and entertainment. Source: Photos courtesy of Academy of Urbanism

twenty years earlier. These strategies are actionable recommendations, but they cannot be tackled in an isolated way; they need to be tackled simultaneously. This urban manifesto is a homage to our beautiful cities, their history and the need to continually re-frame the questions of our urban future. With an agreed set of principles, cities do not need to discuss the obvious at the commencement of every project and reinvent the wheel every time, but can rely on a broadly shared and supported basis and set of strategies.

Urban regeneration is often about incremental change (e.g. the careful repurposing of existing old buildings) and how to embed actions that cumulatively reinforce the existing character of a place (Figs. 1.34 and 1.35).

The Structure of the Book

This book is in many respects a sequel to two previous ones: *The Principles of Green Urbanism* (2010) and *Low Carbon Cities* (2015), both dealing with the link between urban regeneration and sustainable design.

The book is arranged in six chapters. Chapter 1 is an introduction essay that explains the book's approach. The aim of this introductory chapter is to introduce the need for an urban manifesto to regenerate UK cities, summarise the urban challenges and outline the scope of the book.

The *Urban Manifesto for Regenerating UK Cities* (Chap. 5) is underpinned by the thinking and concepts formulated in the three following chapters:

Chapter 2: Reconnecting Cities with Nature
Chapter 3: Understanding the Benefits of Urban Density
Chapter 4: Activating the Food-Water-Energy Nexus

Chapters 2, 3, and 4 elaborate on the different aspects of urban regeneration projects, while the main chapters are Chaps. 5 and 6, which comes in two parts: first, the 'Urban Manifesto with ten strategies' and then thirteen case studies of urban regeneration in UK cities.

The manifesto holistically frames its strategic guidance, and then in the following part makes the case through thirteen selected urban regeneration examples. The chapter explains how the strategies are relevant to urban regeneration, before introducing the thirteen selected cases in UK cities. Thus, the aim of Chap. 5 is to prove that these strategies can be implemented, by discussing recent city regeneration projects and illustrating how these have been put into reality, as exemplified by each of the cases relating directly to the strategies.

The selected cases are all different in scope and scale and are located in the following UK cities (starting in the south and proceeding north):

- Brighton
- Hastings
- Portsmouth
- Bristol
- Cardiff
- Ebbsfleet
- Cambridge
- Birmingham
- Liverpool
- Leeds
- York
- Newcastle upon Tyne
- Glasgow

I am very optimistic about the development of cities in the UK, but we will need to stay focused and innovative. From the *Hotwalls Studios* in Portsmouth, to the *Tobacco Factory* in Bristol, to Glasgow's new *City Campus*—there are amazing urban regeneration projects in different scales happening all over the country that set a high benchmark for future projects to follow. Chapter 6 of this book illustrates some of these selected cases, and how the ten strategies can be adopted and applied. The principles of urban regeneration haven't changed very much over the years—they are the timeless wisdom of good urban design and development that have held true for many decades and will continue to do so for many more decades to come.

References

Alberti, M. (1996). Measuring Urban Sustainability. *Environ Impact Assess Review, 16*, 381–424.

Alexander, C., et al. (1977). *A Pattern Language: Towns, Buildings, Construction*. Center for Environmental Structure Series. New York: Oxford University Press.

Alexander, C., Neis, H., Anninou, A., & King, I. (1987). *A New Theory of Urban Design*. Oxford: Oxford University Press.

Aravena, A. (2018). Notes by Alejandro Aravena as Part of the 16th Architecture Biennale in Venice, Italy; Exhibition Centre Arsenale.

Banham, R. (1969). *The Architecture of the Well-Tempered Environment*. Chicago: University of Chicago Press.

Banham, R. (1976). *Megastructure: Urban Futures of the Recent Past*. New York: Icon (Harper).

Beatley, T. (2014). Imagining Biophilic Cities. In S. Lehmann (Ed.), *Low Carbon Cities*. London: Routledge.

Bennetts Associates. (2018). *Regeneration*. London: Bennetts Associates. Retrieved August 20, 2018, from https://www.bennettsassociates.com/assets/pdf/Regeneration%20booklet_Bennetts%20Associates.pdf.

Bertaud, A., & Malpezzi, S. (2014). *The Spatial Distribution of Population in 57 World Cities* (Draft Paper), University of Wisconsin-Madison.

Bianchini, F., & Parkinson, M. (Eds.). (1993). *Cultural Policy and Urban Regeneration: the West European Experience* (pp. 1–20). Manchester: Manchester University Press.

British Retail Consortium. (2016). Retail Insight and Analytics: Dashboard. Retrieved July 10, 2018, from https://brc.org.uk/.

Brown, L. (2009). *Plan B 4.0: Mobilizing to Save Civilization*. New York: W.W. Norton.

Brundtland, G. H., & Brundtland Commission. (1987). *Our Common Future*. Annex to Report of the World Commission on Environment and Development (WCED), United Nations, Geneva/Oslo. Oxford and New York: Oxford University Press.

Bruns-Berentelg, J. (2018). In Private Conversation with the Author, at HCU Hamburg, on 7 August 2018.

CABE. (2008). *Report: What Makes an Eco-town?* CABE, The UK Government's Commission for Architecture and the Built Environment, London.

Callenbach, E. (1975). *Ecotopia. An Utopian Novel.* New York: Bantam Books.

Cervero, R. (2001). Efficient Urbanization: Economic Performance and the Shape of Metropolis. *Urban Studies, 38*(10), 1651–1671.

Chipperfield, D., & Kretz, S. (2018). Rethinking the Best Use of Spacer. In *Rolex and Architecture*, publication on the occasion of the 16th Biennale of Architecture, Venice, Italy.

Clos, J. (2013). 'Foreword' in UN-Habitat, *Streets as Public Spaces and Drivers of Urban Prosperity*, UN-Habitat, Nairobi, pp. iii–iv.

Cuthbert, A. R. (2006). *The Form of Cities: Political Economy and Urban Design.* Oxford and New York: Blackwell Publishing.

Department of Transport, London. (2018). GB Driving Licence Data (study published 11 April 2018 by DoT). Retrieved July 10, 2018, from https://data.gov.uk/dataset/d0be1ed2-9907-4ec4-b552-c048f6aec16a/gb-driving-licence-data.

Durkheim, E. (1895/2011). *Les règles de la méthode sociologique* (German translation: *Die Regeln der soxziologischen Methode*); Felix Alcan, Paris.

Ehrlich, P. (1968). *The Population Bomb.* New York: Ballantine Books/Random House.

Elmqvist, T., et al. (2018). *The Urban Planet. Knowledge Towards Sustainable Cities.* Cambridge, UK: Cambridge University Press.

Evans, J., & Jones, P. (2008/2nd edn. 2013). *Urban Regeneration in the UK: Boom, Bust and Recovery.* London: Sage Publications.

Ficco, S. (2017). Regional Economic Performance for a Selected Sample of EU Countries. *Europe Economics Blog.* Retrieved November 16, 2017.

Florida, R. (2002). *The Rise of the Creative Class.* New York: Basic Books.

Garreau, J. (1992). *Edge City: Life on the New Frontier.* New York: Penguin Random House.

Gehl, J. (2010). *Life Between Buildings: Using Public Space* (6th ed.). Copenhagen/London: The Danish Architectural Press/Island Press.

Giddens, A. (1999). *Runaway World. How Globalization Is Reshaping Our Lives.* London: Routledge.

Girardet, H. (1999). *Creating Sustainable Cities.* Totnes, Devon: Green Books or the Schumacher Society.

Girardet, H. (2008). *Cities, People, Planet: Urban Development and Climate Change.* (2nd edn. London: John Wiley & Sons.

Glaeser, E. L. (2011). *The Triumph of the City: How Our Greatest Invention Makes Us Richer, Smarter, Greener, Healthier, and Happier.* New York and London: Penguin Press.

Haas, T. (Ed.). (2012). *Sustainable Urbanism and Beyond.* New York: Rizzoli.

Hall, P. (1988). *Cities of Tomorrow: An Intellectual History of Urban Planning and Design in the Twentieth Century.* Oxford and New York: Blackwell.

Hall, P., & Pfeiffer, U. (2000). *Urban Future 21: A Global Agenda for 21st-Century Cities.* New York: E & FN Spon.

Head, P. (2008). *Entering the Ecological Age: The Engineer's Role.* London, UK: Institution of Civil Engineers. Retrieved June 20, 2016, from www.arup.com/Publications/Entering_the_Ecological_Age.aspx.

Hensel, M., & Nilsson, F. (Eds.). (2016). *The Changing Shape of Practice*. London and New York: Routledge.

Hill, J. (2013). Centuries of Design Research. In J. Dehn et al. (Eds.), *When Architects and Designers Write/Draw/Build* (p. 17). Aarhus, Denmark: Arkitektur Forlag.

Howard, E. (1902). *Garden Cities of To-Morrow*. London: Faber & Faber.

Jackson, T. (2009). *Prosperity Without Growth: Economics for a Finite Planet*. London: Earthscan.

Jacobs, J. (1961). *The Death and Life of Great American Cities*. London/New York: Cape/Random House.

Jacobs, A. B. (1995). *Great Streets*. Cambridge, MA: The MIT Press.

Jagger, C., et al. (2016). A Comparison of Health Expectancies Over Two Decades in England. *The Lancet Public Health, 387*, 779–786.

Jagger, C. et al. (2018). Forecasting the Care Needs of the Older Population in England Over the Next 20 Years. *The Lancet Public Health*, August. Retrieved September 1, 2018, from https://www.thelancet.com/journals/lanpub/article/PIIS2468-2667(18)30118-X/fulltext.

Jenks, M., Burton, E., & Williams, K. (Eds.). (1996). *The Compact City: A Sustainable Urban Form*. London: Spon Press.

Koolhaas, R., & Mau, B. (1995). *S,M,L,XL*. New York: Monacelli Press.

Kostof, S. (1999). *The City Shaped: Urban Patterns and Meaning through History* (2nd ed.). London and New York: Thames & Hudson.

Landry, C., Green, L., Matarasso, F., & Bianchini, F. (1996). *The Art of Regeneration: Urban Renewal through Cultural Activity*. Stroud: Comedia.

Le Corbusier. (1933). *Charter of Athens*; Study Undertaken by Le Corbusier and the Congress International d' Architecture Moderne (CIAM), Paris.

Leary, M. E. (Ed.). (2013). *The Routledge Companion to Urban Regeneration*. London and New York: Routledge.

Lehmann, S. (2010). *The Principles of Green Urbanism. Transforming the City for Sustainability*. Chinese edition 2014. London: Earthscan from Routledge.

Lehmann, S. (2012). The Metabolism of the City: Optimizing Urban Material Flow Through Principles of Zero Waste and Sustainable Consumption. In S. Lehmann & R. Crocker (Eds.), *Designing for Zero Waste: Consumption, Technologies and the Built Environment*. London: Routledge.

Lehmann, S. (Ed.). (2015a). *Low Carbon Cities. Transforming Urban Systems*. London: Routledge.

Lehmann, S. (2015b). Low Carbon Cities: More Than Just Buildings. In S. Lehmann (Ed.), *Low Carbon Cities: Transforming Urban Systems* (pp. 1–55). London: Routledge.

Lehmann, S. (2015c). Green Urbanism: From Fossil-Fuel Dependent Cities to Sustainable Eco-cities. In T. Haas & K. Olsson (Eds.), *Urbanisms*. Stockholm: Nordic Academic Press.

Lehmann, S. (2016). Sustainable Urbanism: Towards a Framework for Quality and Optimal Density? *Future Cities and Environment, 2*(8), 1–29. Springer Open (5 August 2016), 1–29. https://doi.org/10.1186/s40984-016-0021-3.

Lehmann, S. (2018). Regenerating the UK's Post-industrial Cities. *CIRIA Network Blog*. London (08 May 2018). Retrieved August 20, 2018, from https://www.ciria.org/News/blog/Regenerating_the_UKs_post_industrial_cities.aspx.

Lehmann, S., Zaman, A., Devlin, J., & Holyoak, N. (2013). Supporting Urban Planning of Low-Carbon Precincts: Integrated Demand Forecasting. *Journal of Sustainability, 5*(12), 5289–5318. https://doi.org/10.3390/su5125289.

Leyden, K. M. (2003). Social Capital and the Built Environment: The Importance of Walkable Neighborhoods. *American Journal of Public Health, 93*(9), 1546–1551. https://doi.org/10.2105/AJPH.93.9.1546.

Lynch, K. (1960). *Image of the City*. Cambridge, MA: MIT Press.

Lynch, K. (1981). *A Theory of Good City Form*. Cambridge, MA: MIT Press.

Madanipur, A. (2003). *Public and Private Spaces of the City*. London: Routledge.

Mau, B. (2004). *Massive Change. A Manifesto for the Future of Global Design*. London and Munich: Phaidon.

McDonough, W., & Braungart, M. (1992). *The Hannover Principles: Design for Sustainability*. Report Commissioned by the Hannover EXPO, Germany. Available online.

McDonough, W., & Braungart, M. (2002). *Cradle to Cradle: Remaking the Way We Make Things* (1st ed.). New York, NY: North Point Press.

Meadows, D. H., Meadows, D. L., Randers, J., & Behrens, W. (1972). *The Limits to Growth: A Report to the Club of Rome's Project on the Predicament of Mankind*. New York, NY/Washington, DC: Universe Books/Pontomac Books (1971 Report/1972 Book).

Melvin, J. (2018). Rubs in Urbe, Unpacked: On Countryside Running Through the Heart of English Cities. *Architectural Review*, April 2018 Issue on Rethinking the Rural, London.

Mostafavi, M., & Doherty, G. (Eds.). (2010). *Ecological Urbanism*. Baden, Switzerland: Lars Mueller.

Mumford, L. (1962). *The City in History: Its Origins, Its Transformations, and Its Prospects*. New York: Harcort, Brace & World Inc.

Muthesius, H. (1908). *Das Englische Haus*. Berlin: Gebr. Mann Verlag.

O'Connor, S. (2018). Cities Only Work If They Accommodate Rich and Poor. Article in *Financial Times*, London, UK (20 March 2018). Retrieved July 10, 2018, from https://www.ft.com/content/4f7c158a-2b66-11e8-9b4b-bc4b9f08f381.

OECD. (2012). *Compact City Policies. A Comparative Assessment*. Paris: OECD Publishing.

Papanek, V. (1984). *Design for the Real World: Human Ecology and Social Change* (2nd rev. ed.). London: Thames and Hudson.

Rasmussen, S. E. (1962). *Experiencing Architecture*. Cambridge, MA: The MIT Press.

Rees, W., & Wackernagel, M. (1994). Ecological Footprints and Appropriated Carrying Capacity: Measuring the Natural Capital Requirements of the Human Economy. In A. M. Jansson, M. Hammer, C. Folke, & R. Costanza (Eds.), *Investing in Natural Capital: The Ecological Economics Approach to Sustainability*. Washington, DC: Island Press.

Register, R. (1987). *Eco-City Berkeley: Building Cities for a Healthy Future*. Boston: North Atlantic Books.

Roberts, P., Skyes, H., & Granger, R. (2016). *Urban Regeneration: A Handbook* (2nd ed.). London: Sage Publications.

Rowe, C., & Koetter, F. (1978). *Collage City*. Cambridge, MA: MIT Press.

Santamouris, M., et al. (Eds.). (2001). *Energy and Climate in the Urban Built Environment*. London: James & James.

Schwarz, L. (2000). London: 1700–1840. In P. Clark (Ed.), *The Cambridge Urban History of Britain (No. 2)*. Cambridge: Cambridge University Press.

Sidewalk Labs Project, Alphabet (Google), Toronto; see www.sidewalklabs.com.

Smyth, H. (1994). *Marketing the City: the Role of Flagship Developments in Urban Regeneration*. London: E & FN Spon.

Szokolay, S. (2004). *Introduction to Architectural Science*. Oxford/London: Architectural Press/Elsevier Science.

Talberth, J., Cobb, C., & Slattery, N. (2006). *The Genuine Progress Indicator 2006: A Tool for Sustainable Development*. Oakland, CA: Redefining Progress. Retrieved November 27, 2017, from www.rprogress.org.

The United Nations. (2015). Sustainable Development Goals (SDGs), Geneva. Retrieved July 10, 2018, from www.un.org/sustainabledevelopment/sustainable-development-goals/.

The United Nations. (2016). The New Urban Agenda; Habitat III, Quito (Oct. 2016). Available online.

The Urban Task Force, & Rogers, R. (1999). *Towards an Urban Renaissance* (Report, June 1999). London: UTF/DETR and E & FN Spon. Available online.

The World Bank. (2010). *Cities and Climate Change: An Urgent Agenda*. Washington, DC: World Bank.

Travers, T., Sims, S., & Bosetti, N. (2016). *Housing and Inequality in London*. Report Published by Centre for London, UK (April 2016).

UN EP. (2011). *Decoupling Natural Resource Use and Environmental Impacts from Economic Growth: A Report of the Working Group on Decoupling to the International Resource Panel*, M. Fischer-Kowalski, M. Swilling, E. U. von Weizsäcker, Y. Ren, Y. Moriguchi, W. Crane, F. Krausmann, N. Eisenmenger, S. Giljum, P. Hennicke, P. Romero Lankao, & A. Siriban Manalang (Eds.). Paris: UNEP-Sustainable Consumption and Production Branch.

UN EP. (2013). *City-Level Decoupling: Urban Resource Flows and the Governance of Infrastructure Transitions*. A Report of the Working Group on Cities of the International Resource Panel. Authors include: Swilling, M., Robinson, B., Marvin, S., & Hodson, M. Retrieved March 10, 2017, from http://web.unep.org/ourplanet/october2016/unep-publications/city-level-decoupling.

URBED. (2005). *Better Neighbourhoods: Making Higher Density Work*. London: CABE, p. 28.

Urry, J. (2011). *Climate Change and Society*. Cambridge: Polity Press.

Von Weizaecker, E., Lovins, A., & Lovins, H. (1997). *Factor Four: Doubling Wealth, Halving Resource Use*. London: Earthscan.

Wheeler, S., & Beatley, T. (Eds.). (2004). *The Sustainable Urban Development Reader*. Oxford: Routledge.

Whyte, W. (1980). *The Social Life of Small Spaces*. Washington, DC: Conservation Foundation.

Wilson, E. O. (1984). *The Biophilia Hypothesis*. New York: Island Press.

2

Reconnecting Cities with Nature, Building Resilience at the Urban Scale

Unsustainable, non-resilient urbanisation patterns and the neglect of inner-city urban areas have caused fragmentation, depletion and urban decline, led to humankind overpowering nature, causing biodiversity loss and the degradation of ecosystems and their services. Urban regeneration projects allow us to 'repair' and restore some of this damage while enhancing urban resilience. For instance, increasing connectivity between existing and enhanced ecosystems and restoring them within cities and at the peri-urban fringe (e.g. through nature-based solutions and the re-naturing of neighbourhoods) is necessary to strengthen ecosystem resilience and the adaptive capacity to cope with the effects of climate change. There is growing recognition of the need for daily contact with green spaces and nature in order to live happy, productive and meaningful lives.

How can we arrive at a better relationship between nature and the built environment, in a symbiotic coexistence? As laid out in this chapter, transforming the existing city and neighbourhoods in the described way will enable ecosystems to deliver their services for more liveable and healthier cities.

© The Author(s) 2019
S. Lehmann, *Urban Regeneration*, https://doi.org/10.1007/978-3-030-04711-5_2

The Seriousness and Urgency Caused by Global Warming

With global warming and the impacts of climate change, we will need to seriously rethink how our cities should evolve to become more resilient and resource-efficient. A group of leading scientists are warning of grim prospects if we keep abusing the planet, and that the commitment of the Paris Agreement (2016) to keep warming at two degrees Celsius above pre-industrial levels may not be enough to 'park' the planet's climate trajectory at a stable temperature.

Jonathan Watts described the 'domino-effect of climate events' that could move the Earth into a hothouse state, arguing that leading scientists warned that passing such a point would make efforts to reduce emissions increasingly futile (2018). The loss of the Greenland ice sheet could disrupt the Gulf Stream, which would in turn raise sea levels and accelerate Antarctic ice loss, triggering a domino-like cascade of melting ice, warming seas, shifting currents, dying forests and releasing of methane trapped in Siberian permafrost that could tilt the Earth into a 'hothouse' state (that is 4C warmer than pre-industrial times) beyond which human efforts to reduce emissions will be increasingly impossible. In 'Losing Earth', Nathaniel Rich writes (2018, p. 2):

> If by some miracle we are able to limit global warming to two degrees Celsius, we will only have to negotiate the extinction of the world's tropical reefs, sea-level rise of several meters and the abandonment of the Persian Gulf. The climate scientist James Hansen has called two-degree warming "a prescription for long-term disaster." Long-term disaster is now the best-case scenario. Three-degree warming is a prescription for short-term disaster: forests in the Arctic and the loss of most coastal cities. Robert Watson, a former director of the United Nations Intergovernmental Panel on Climate Change, has argued that three-degree warming is the realistic minimum. Four degrees: Europe in permanent drought; vast areas of China, India and Bangladesh claimed by desert; Polynesia swallowed by the sea; the Colorado River thinned to a trickle; the American Southwest largely uninhabitable.

With this in mind, it is obvious: climate change is not something in a faraway future but is already around us and impacting on our daily lives. All this has created an urgency that means we will have to deal with our cities in a different way.

For too long we have ignored the relevance of climate change viewed through its links to globalisation, capitalism and social injustice. The topic has lost our interest because it appears too large for us to be able to do something about. Eco-philosopher Timothy Morton (2007) calls this phenomenon a 'hyperobject': a challenge that is too big and complex to grasp or take action on, because we cannot see its interconnections with other areas such as social injustice; everybody simply continues and pretends as if the challenge simply does not exist. This is why it is essential to connect the climate change debate with issues of social injustice. We have to ask what the alternative model to our form of capitalism could be.

Instead of trying to use the idea of nature existing to heal what society has damaged, Morton has a deep understanding of ecology that sets out a radical new form of ecological criticism that he calls 'dark ecology'. He argues that the chief stumbling block to environmental thinking is the image of nature itself and the ecological catastrophe in which we continue to live. French philosopher and sociologist Bruno Latour argues (2015) that an entire new world view and thought model is necessary, one that deals with the links between climate change and our economic system, the promise of progress, and the conflicts created by migration.

Our Disconnect from Nature: The Era of the Anthropocene

Humankind is not only actively reshaping the world but the impact of human activity is so pronounced that it is changing the behaviour of our planet. The aim is to arrive at a symbiotic coexistence that creates a spatial experience which heightens and deepens our awareness of the environment.

One important characteristic of complex urban systems is their resilience. Urban resilience of cities means the ability to maintain human and ecosystem functions simultaneously over the long-term (Alberti and Marzluff 2004). Urban resilience, also called *adaptive capacity*, refers to a city's ability to cope with and recover quickly from hardship or crisis. A resilient city is typically one that is prepared and well-equipped to contend with and mitigate the multiple effects of climate change, such as urban heat islands, heatwaves, urban flooding, energy blackouts and potential disasters. A resilient city has a robust infrastructural system and can even turn a crisis into a positive development (Mitchell and Harris 2012; Meerow et al. 2016).

Redefining cities in the age of global warming goes right to the core of our ability to adapt, and underpins our complicated relationship with nature, technology and place. For some time now humankind has been out of touch with nature and has lost its connection to the natural world. There is a need for us to renew our connection with nature since this is key to both good health and resilience. Related to this is the importance of re-greening cities and introducing nature-based solutions through urban regeneration projects.

Biodiversity evolves as different species share the same ecosystem where relationships between the species develop. Each species is necessary for keeping something in balance in the natural world. In this balanced system, the planet's biodiversity has grown to include 30 million different species. Early humans, only emerged around 200,000 years ago. We are a comparatively young species!

Can humans really be the most advanced species on Earth? All of this time, hunting and gathering has been what we do best. Since the time of the dinosaurs 65 million years ago, there has not been this level of sustained destruction on our planet. The current rapid loss of biodiversity is quite possibly the biggest disaster ever. In the big picture of Earth's evolution, *homo sapiens* has only been around for a very short time, and it is likely that the Earth will still be around for a long time even after we have destroyed ourselves as a species.

But today, a new awareness is emerging that is driving the regeneration and re-greening of our cities. Humans are able to and have a desire to participate in the community of life and in nature, interacting with all of the species on this planet, without necessarily destroying any of it, let alone destroying all of it. The Earth is probably less than 4.5 billion years old and life has been around on this planet for 3.8 billion years, starting right at the beginning with single-cell organisms. Very early on in this evolution we find photosynthesis, which causes the planet to rapidly change. As a consequence the atmosphere begins to change and we see biodiversity developing, with 'terra firma' becoming colonized by plants, insects and mammals.

We, as such a young species, could learn to live on the planet by studying nature. *Homo sapiens* means 'wise man' after all. Over the last 35,000 years, we have been gradually pulling back from nature. Around this time we see the first cave paintings and simple tools being developed. Aboriginal Australians are still living proof of this period. They represent 50,000 years of uninterrupted living culture, based on the 'touching the Earth lightly' concept, meaning that you only take from nature what you really need at that particular moment. But then, around

10,000 years ago, we woke up to the cycles and seasons of nature, and in this process we saw the opportunity to become farmers. This has been a process of empowering ourselves and taking control of our own lives and our own destiny. The emergence of *homo sapiens* has shifted the global balance and led to a new understanding of nature: We are not at the mercy of nature; we can farm the land, build dwellings that resist nature's forces, and we can harness what agriculture offers.

Everything changed again with scientific discovery, technology and the Industrial Revolution. Over the last 300 years we saw that we could manipulate nature through the emergence of science. Humankind started to believe that it had dominion over the Earth; and that the Earth and nature have to serve us in our own evolution. Just think of the discoveries of philosophers and scientists like Copernicus, Galileo, Descartes and Newton. Their understanding was that nature was meaningless and purposeless, and its only function was to 'serve humans in their evolution'. Descartes for instance believed that animals had no feelings. His belief was: 'Man is at the top and Earth is here for us to use, to exploit' (see Fig. 2.2).

83 per cent of the UK's population currently live in urban areas, and a large portion are estranged from nature. We have changed how we live. Today, 90 percent of our lives is spent indoors, in controlled interior environments. Within a very short time, humans experienced a transition of existence from life predominantly spent outside towards a very different life inside buildings.

A fundamental break with nature was the result. If we put it in proportion, everything about how we define ourselves today, our cities, industries and our technologies, have only been on Earth for the blink of an eye. All this time we have been constantly pulling back from nature; we have seen ourselves increasingly as separate from and superior to nature. Over thousands of years we have been empowering ourselves as humankind, but in this process have been pulling back from the natural world, losing our connection to nature. That process has gone so far now that we are running into an 'evolutionary wall'. Despite all the science we still treat animals as if they are nothing and have no feelings—just think of battery farms, or animal experiments in the cosmetics industry.

The seminal book 'The limits to growth' (Meadows and Club of Rome 1972) displayed the limits of finite resources and noted that the whole Industrial Revolution was about taking and extracting minerals and resources, and disposing of waste, with a complete disregard for the environment (see Fig. 2.1).

Fig. 2.1 The linear extraction process of resources is unsustainable. Source: Graph supplied by the author

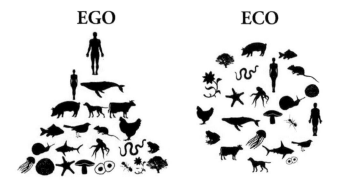

Fig. 2.2 'Ego-Eco'—Humankind is part of the ecosystem, not apart from or above it. This diagram depicts this simple fact clearly. Source: Graph supplied by the author

Walkable Neighbourhoods and the Ability to Enjoy Nature Within the City

Today, we are at a turning point: we understand that cities need to be built on regenerative principles, as we start to grasp how everything in life and the environment is connected. We are revisiting the wisdom of nature to inform our organisational structures (e.g. local food production) and realise that nature has a profound positive influence on our health and well-being. Reconnecting with nature makes people come alive and nourishes the senses.

The only way, if we are ever to make it as a species on this planet, is to reconnect with nature. Today, we have arrived at this new understanding, that we are merely participants in the natural world. We rediscover indigenous traditions and the interdependence of all things in nature, things which coexist together. The inter-connectedness of things—it means that we are not in a privileged position to exploit or destroy the ecosystem. In fact the opposite is true. We have a position of stewardship, where we must lead in a respectful and responsible relationship to the natural world. We are not 'above' nature.

In 1850, Alexander von Humboldt described the cosmos in great detail. However, Charles Darwin's theory 'On the Origin of Species' (1859) was very different. Some people claim that our understanding of nature took a wrong turn when Darwin's vision of natural selection, which was very compatible with the competitive capitalistic ideology of late Victorian England, prevailed over Humboldt's more systemic vision. Csikszentmihalyi notes that 'The Victorian milieu might have recognised itself in Darwin's theory and encouraged naturalists to adopt it as the dogma of biology' (1997, p. 423) (Fig. 2.2).

The study of ecology allows for an understanding of the Earth as a single living system that is in balance. Within this system, cities evolve as the greatest creation of humankind. However, cities are also a source of overload and environmental stress. Cities can possess degrading conditions—just think of windowless work environments, over-crowded housing, air pollution and noise.

The quality of our social, professional and ecological relationships is at the core of what makes us feel alive, happy and safe. Part of this are walkable neighbourhoods on a human scale and the ability to enjoy nature within the city.

Urban designers worldwide aim to bring nature back into the city, to compensate for a lack of parks, gardens and green spaces in cities. Today, we talk about the concept of 'Urban Metabolism', a model which understands cities as a living organism. Urban metabolism analyses the flows of energy, resources, food, people and materials in cities (as if the city were an ecosystem) and provides a framework for the study of the interactions of natural and human systems, using the metaphor of the city as a living organism. Ecologist Arthur George Tansley (1871–1955) expanded the term in 1935 to encompass the material and energetic streams (Tansley 1935). Seminal texts by different authors offer further ecological wisdom on the architect's relationship with landscapes and their ecosystems (Carson 1962; McHarg 1969; Register 1987; McDonough and Braungart 2002; Girardet 2008).

Climate change is caused by humans, through the production of heat-trapping greenhouse gases caused by carbon-dioxide. We have changed the whole dynamics of the planet in a very short time, and we have disrupted billions of years of evolution. Earth was always able to regulate itself, self-regulating the temperature and weather system—fragile systems which have now fallen out of balance. The complex interactive, self-regulating system of biosphere, geosphere and atmosphere has become messed up by global warming and the dangerous effects of climate change. We have been destroying billions of years of creativity and evolution that enabled all of the vitality on Earth to co-exist side-by-side. However, we are just awakening to this mistake; the Earth and nature are not things to dominate and exploit, but a community we are to be part of, to enjoy and participate in.

A new deep understanding of nature has emerged that sees the commonality of all of life as part of the same ecosystem, and it influences our thinking of cities as living organisms (one of these approaches is 'urban metabolism'). The concept that the Earth is a self-correcting organism, the so-called *Gaia hypothesis*, was developed by James E. Lovelock in 1975 and published in 1979. It states that the Earth is a vulnerable system in balance, and that the temperature of the planet and its atmosphere are produced and maintained by the sum of living organisms. The Gaia hypothesis is based on the idea that the life of earth functions as a single system which actually defines and maintains conditions necessary for its survival. Lovelock argues that the earth's living matter—air, ocean and land surfaces—forms a complex system which has the capacity to keep our planet a fit place for life.

The Gaia hypothesis has fundamentally altered the way scientists view evolution and the environment, but not all agree. Contrary to the Gaia hypothesis, which suggests the Earth has a self-righting tendency, Johan Rockstroem (Director of the Stockholm Resilience Centre, 2018) and numerous other leading scientists say that the feedbacks of global warming could push the planet to a more extreme state (Figs. 2.3 and 2.4).

From Garden Cities to Biophilia: Healthy Cities

Numbers of cases of diabetes, obesity, depression and dementia are on a steep rise, which poses the question why it can be so unhealthy to live in certain cities. A *healthy city* is conscious of the health of its residents and strives to improve it. Thus, a healthy city has a strong commitment to health and wellbeing, and a process to achieve it. The WHO report (2014) refers to the need for sufficient

Figs. 2.3 and 2.4 There are numerous ways greenery and vegetation can be integrated in buildings, for instance, such as this hanging gardens in Singapore. Source: Photos supplied by the author. Green space and the urban are no contradiction, but can co-exist side by side, as here in Rotterdam. Source: Photos supplied by the author

green spaces in cities and defines what a *Healthy City* is: 'A healthy city is one that continually creates and improves its physical and social environments and expands the community resources that enable people to mutually support each other in performing all the functions of life and developing to their maximum potential.' This approach puts health high on the political and social agenda of cities and builds a strong movement for public health at the local level. It strongly emphasizes equity, participatory governance and solidarity, inter-sectoral collaboration and action to address the determinants of urban health. The concept of Healthy Cities was inspired and supported by the *WHO European Health for All* strategy and the Health21 targets and is aligned with the UN's 2030 Agenda for Sustainable Development.

English towns and cities have a long tradition of integrating nature in the form of parks and gardens into the urban context. As mentioned earlier, English urbanism and the Garden City concept, has never set the urban above the rural. The rural was always the place of *Arcadia* where the traditional English family would like to live, almost an anti-urban concept. So it comes as no surprise that green spaces and various forms of the countryside were always running through the heart of old

English cities, with towns penetrated by fields, orchards, meadows and fish ponds. The compelling vision of a self-sufficient garden city aimed to combine the advantages of both urban and rural living (Howard 1902).

As predicted by Rachel Carson in 'Silent Spring' in 1962, we are now in the process of redefining our relationship with nature, and how our lives depend upon it. This new understanding is not about giving up technology, but rather developing the most advanced technologies to date, for instance through the biological revolution and nanotechnology. We have to use that rich and available knowledge to find new and better solutions, employing ideas of 'biomimicry' (Benyus 2002; Neves and Francke 2012).

The emulation of nature's genius is a promising path for our urban systems, processing and neighbourhood designs. It goes beyond just emulating natural form, involving systems' thinking and asking: how does it fit into the wider ecosystem? Nature has 3.8 billion years of R&D behind it, which we can learn from. Learning from nature also means that the principles of a Circular Economy have become part of this learning process. The Ellen McArthur Foundation (EMF) argues that 'a circular economy is one that is restorative and regenerative by design' (2017). Part of the circular economy includes designing out waste and rebuilding natural capital and resilience. In order to support this, the EMF has published a series of key texts on the circular economy that are freely available online (Figs. 2.5 and 2.6).

What does this all mean for the urban regeneration of our cities? This urban manifesto envisions the rise of regenerative city design and planning based on the

Figs. 2.5 and 2.6 English towns and cities have a long tradition of integrating nature in form of parks and gardens into the urban context. Source: Open source images

concepts of urban metabolism and the principles of a circular economy. The question must be: how can we create public spaces, infrastructure, buildings, neighbourhoods and products without destroying nature and the ecosystem?

There is significant potential for a new technological era inspired by nature. We can improve the cooling of buildings by looking at the natural world for solutions, for instance we can harness the process of photosynthesis. Solar power, CO_2 and water create—in the process of photosynthesis—energy and oxygen. This is relevant, as we have to ask: could we pull CO_2 out of the atmosphere in this way, for example by planting more urban forests in all cities?

It is well documented that there is enough solar energy every day to power all of our cities. All of regenerative city thinking is also relevant for human health, by providing clean air, clean water, and vibrant local foods from the natural environment around us. Instead, it is tragic what is happening to our forests and oceans. For instance, it is well documented that plastic waste leads to toxins entering our bodies through the food chain.

There is also increasing evidence of the health benefits from re-greening our cities: for instance, a faster healing process from illness. If we have hospitals with a window view into a garden, this enables faster recovery from surgery. It relates to the concept of 'Biophilia', nature's restorative, regenerative capacity. This includes the benefits for children of being in nature on a daily basis (Wilson 1984; Kellert 2011). The 'Biophilia hypothesis' has first been introduced by Edward O. Wilson in 1984, suggesting that 'humans possess an innate tendency to seek connections with nature and other forms of life'. Biophilia explores the various ways of greening and re-naturing cities to strengthen the calming and cooling effect of nature, and the improvement of air quality and microclimate.

This is timely, as a recent survey (*BBC News* 2018, reporting on a WHO study) has revealed that 47 UK towns and cities exceed air pollution limits and have an unhealthy environment to live in! The WHO study found that 30 areas in the UK have fine-particle air pollution levels above 10 micrograms per cubic metre, with another 17 at that limit. Areas that exceeded the level included London, Manchester, Swansea, Leeds, Leicester, Liverpool, Nottingham, Plymouth and Sheffield (beside others). Fine-particle air pollution is particularly bad for us, penetrating deep into the lungs and cardiovascular system, causing diseases including stroke, heart disease, lung cancer and respiratory infections.

But if the outside air has become so polluted, the 'open the window' cooling option is less viable and resolution is sought from air-conditioning systems, this creates further energy needs, generating more heat, emissions and pollution.

Stephen Kellert noted (2011): 'Biophilic Design is an innovative way of designing the places where we live, work, and learn. We need nature in a deep and fundamental fashion, but we have often designed our cities and suburbs in ways that both degrade the environment and alienate us from nature. The recent trend in green architecture has decreased the environmental impact of the built environment, but it has accomplished little in the way of reconnecting us to the natural world, the missing piece in the puzzle of sustainable development.'

In the urban regeneration process, ideally we want to increase the density of UK cities and increase access to urban green space. Increasing the amount of urban greenery and facilitating access to urban green space while at the same time increasing urban density is not a contradiction, but a smart strategy that is feasible, as currently demonstrated by a number of large regeneration projects, from Barcelona to Singapore. Malmo in Sweden has positively branded itself as the 'City of Parks', and Singapore calls itself the 'City in a Garden'.

In today's fast-paced, over-loaded and distracting built environment, places of refuge, escape and relaxation are much needed within the city (with easy access) to separate ourselves from the external world. Children are masters in identifying and enjoying such 'secret places', and in finding joyous moments in pocket spaces and intimate gardens.

Biodiversity Loss and Ecosystem Degradation: What Can Urban Planners and Landscape Designers Do?

Urban expansion is leading to changes of the UK countryside, shifting green space to 'artificial surfaces'. An aerial survey of the UK in 2015 revealed that over 22,000 hectares of green space was converted to artificial surfaces between 2006 and 2012. Over 7000 hectares were converted from forest to artificial surfaces, and over 14,000 hectares changed from agricultural areas and farmland to artificial surfaces. Over 1000 hectares were converted from wetlands to artificial surfaces in order to provide more space for households. Completion of construction sites in urban areas made up nearly 3000 hectares and completed new industrial and commercial developments just over 1000 hectares (report by the University of Leicester 2015).

After a long period of inactivity, the UK Government is now trying to quickly fix the issue of housing affordability by boosting supply and approving inacceptable housing developments on precious greenfield land. However, far too many homes are being planned and built on greenfield sites that were formerly protected green-belt land. There are sufficient brownfield sites for an extra two million homes in England alone, and there is no excuse for further encroaching into precious greenfield land that is necessary for recreation, biodiversity, forestry and food supply. The redevelopment of brownfield land and infill densification is still not prioritised enough by the government, developers and policy makers.

Established in 1955 by Patrick Abercrombie and others, the *Green Belt* policy was intended to halt urban sprawl by marking a green ring of protected countryside around cities and towns against 'inappropriate development'. The size of the green belt is estimated at 1.63 million hectares, about 13 percent of the land area of England. It is concentrated around the largest cities, but extends to many smaller cities and towns.

UK cities are facing a broad range of challenges, such as unsustainable urbanisation (frequently at too low density) and related human health issues, degradation and loss of natural capital and the ecosystem services it provides (clean air, water and soil), climate change and an alarming increase in natural disaster risks.

Obviously trees and their canopies are a critical piece of the life support system on this planet and are vital for any future project. Urban forest projects, constructed wetlands and the urban farming movement are all good ways to re-integrate nature into an urban setting. Part of this are green roofs, living walls and vegetated pergolas (see Fig. 2.7).

Natural elements such as street trees, gardens and planting have been a feature of cities for hundreds of years. The most effective urban green space is not a lawn, but a garden with tree coverage from different types of trees and bushes. As far back as his 1722 book, 'The City Gardener', the English botanist Thomas Fairchild (1667–1729) noted that city residents feel more relaxed and healthy when they can enjoy gardens and greenery (Fairchild 1722). He suggested to improve air pollution and improve the urban micro-climate in London by creating parks and gardens, and he also realised that numerous small gardens with trees and bushes are more effective

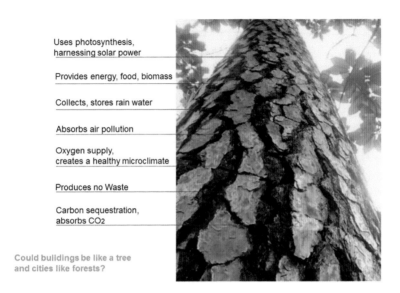

Uses photosynthesis,
harnessing solar power

Provides energy, food, biomass

Collects, stores rain water

Absorbs air pollution

Oxygen supply,
creates a healthy microclimate

Produces no Waste

Carbon sequestration,
absorbs CO2

Could buildings be like a tree
and cities like forests?

Fig. 2.7 A tree knows no waste, but provides a large range of ecosystem services. Source: Photo supplied by the author

rather than just a large park with a lawn. Almost three hundred years later, the research on the urban heat island (UHI) effect confirms Fairchild's observation.

The dangerous UHI effect leads to significantly warmer urban areas compared to surrounding rural areas, and this temperature difference is usually larger at night than during the day. The UHI effect occurs because the dense, dark surfaces (such as bitumen on roads and concrete on building roofs) absorb and store heat during the day and then release it at night. Urban greenery can help reduce this heat gain and the impact on human health (Sailor 2014; Lehmann 2015). The main cause of the urban heat island effect is from the modification of land surfaces and material, for instance concrete roofs that store and trap solar heat during the day. It can best be counteracted by green roofs (and facades) with planting and vegetation, white or light-coloured surfaces (using the albedo effect to reflect solar radiation) and the use of materials that absorb less heat (Note: from 2012 to 2014, the author was principal investigator of 'Urban Climate Research', the largest study of the UHI effect in Australian cities). It is only a question of time until green roofs will become mandatory for new buildings in the UK.

Understanding the many benefits of urban greening, municipalities are now looking at how urban areas can adapt their landscapes to better cope with increasing heat stress and the urban heat island effect. There is growing recognition and awareness that re-naturing cities can help provide viable solutions for urban engineering that use and deploy the properties of natural ecosystems and the services that they provide. Ecosystem services that city vegetation delivers, through avenues, gardens, parks, wetlands, urban forests, green roofs and living walls are much celebrated. These 'nature-based solutions' (NBS) can provide sustainable, cost-effective and flexible alternatives for various urban planning objectives; working with nature, rather than against it, can further pave the way towards a more resource efficient, competitive and greener economy (what is often termed 'green growth'). It can also help to enhance the natural capital rather than deplete it.

The term 'nature-based solutions' refers to the use of nature for tackling environmental and societal challenges while increasing biodiversity. A definition offered by the European Union Commission, who has been funding some of our research in NBS, states that these solutions 'inspired and supported by nature, which are cost-effective, simultaneously provide environmental, social and economic benefits and help build resilience (…) and bring more, and more diverse, nature and natural features and processes into cities, landscapes and seascapes, through locally adapted, resource-efficient and systemic interventions' (EU-Commission 2015, 2017).

For instance, green roofs or walls can be used to reduce the impact of high temperatures, capture storm water, abate pollution and fine dust, and act as carbon sinks, while enhancing biodiversity. Similarly, the collection and storage of rain water in constructed wetlands, or the protection of mangrove forests along coastlines utilise a nature-based solution to accomplish several things, including disaster risk reduction. Urban flood control is regulated in a natural way, and mangroves moderate the impact of waves and wind on coastal settlements or cities while sequestering CO_2. Additionally, the mangrove forests can provide safe nurseries for marine life and help control coastal erosion resulting from sea-level rise, mitigating and repairing potentially harmful effects on the environment and on human health and society (Lennon and Scott 2014; Maes and Jacobs 2015; Kabisch et al. 2016).

Architects and planners are now increasingly engaged in the thoughtful process of reversing the ecological change process they have caused in the first place, using nature-based solutions to 'repair' the damaged ecosystems. Repair can happen through remediation of industrial land, cleaning of polluted soil or the careful reuse of existing—it is central to enabling urban health and social, cultural and economic regeneration.

When it comes to urban growth and development, we should learn from the metaphor of a garden. The 'natural' form for sustainable urbanisation is no longer exclusively the grid, which was right when infrastructure came in metal pipes (Falk 2018). New organic urban design concepts should guide the inclusion and re-introduction of greenery and biodiversity in the urban built environment. Preserving biodiversity in the face of urbanisation, habitat fragmentation, environmental degradation and climate change is one of the greatest challenges of our time. The integration of trees, shrubs and flora into green spaces and gardens in the city is particularly important in helping to keep the built environment cool, because buildings and pavements increase heat absorption and heat storage, causing the urban heat island effect.

Numerous studies have recently been conducted on the role of green canopies in urban life, with the result that tree coverage differs widely between cities. For instance, in 2018 the *MIT Senseable City Lab* established the *Green View Index* (GVI) that represents the total percentage of a city covered by trees. The study found that Paris has a very high population density but only a GVI of 8.7 percent, compared to London (12.7 percent), Amsterdam (20.6) or Oslo (28.8 percent) (Senseable City Lab, MIT 2018).

Tomorrow's urban neighbourhoods will have to offer new forms of green spaces, both for recreation and to mitigate the warmer urban microclimate. In addition, future neighbourhoods will have to generate at least half of their power themselves. Integrated development with a focus on energy and water management, greenery and the urban microclimate will assume a lead role in urban regeneration. A good example for this trend is Australia's largest urban renewal projects, *Barangaroo* waterfront development at East Darling Harbour in Sydney. At Barangaroo, all roofscapes are green roofs, contributing to the mitigation of the urban heat island effect and collecting rainwater; 40 per cent of the site is open public space, and this inner-city precinct is already setting new standards for Australian urban renewal. Similar to *HafenCity* in Hamburg, the developers use landscaping to deal with flood protection (see Fig. 2.8).

Measuring the Value of Nature: Natural Capital

Climate change has shifted from being viewed as a problem of reducing greenhouse gas emissions incrementally and adapting to specific impacts, to a challenge that requires fundamental transformation in order to achieve all three: liveability, decarbonisation and resilience.

Fig. 2.8 Barangaroo in Sydney is Australia's largest urban regeneration project. Source: Courtesy of Lend Lease, Sydney; supplied by the author

'Natural capital' is the world's stock of natural assets, which include geology, soil, air, water and all living things. It is from this natural capital that humans are able to derive a wide range of services, called 'ecosystem services'. These services make life possible and include water supply, food and biomass supply, clean air supply, energy supply, carbon storage and sequestration, flood control, natural medicines, and so on. There are also many less visible ecosystem services such as climate regulation, the pollination of crops by insects, and natural flood defences provided by mangrove forests, as well as the inspiration and well-being we take from the natural environment (Hawken et al. 1999) (see Fig. 2.9).

The World Forum on Natural Capital explains why our natural capital debt is an issue: 'With natural capital, when we draw down too much stock from our natural environment we also run up a debt which needs to be paid back, for example by replanting clear-cut forests, or allowing aquifers to replenish themselves after we have abstracted water. If we keep drawing down stocks of natural capital without allowing or encouraging nature to recover, we run the risk of local, regional or even global ecosystem collapse' (2018).

Food supply is a significant part of our natural system, and ideas for urban farming, hydroponics and aquaponics have emerged as viable strategies to integrate food production into the urban context. For instance, introducing small-scale residential aquaponics systems would ensure that our growing cities can feed themselves in a healthy and sustainable way with locally grown food. Aquaponics is a soil-free closed-loop natural system that pumps the nutrient-rich waste water from fish farming to nourish green leafy vegetable crops growing in water bays. Aquaponic farms can easily be integrated into every city block or neighbourhood,

Nature-based solutions
Ecosystem Services

Clean
Air

CO2
NO2
Storage

Flood
control

Shadow
&
Humidity

Bio
Diversity

Water
Cycle

Food &
Bio
Mass   Ecosystem Services
            from Green Infrastructure

Fig. 2.9 Eco-system services include numerous essential services provided by nature, such as water management and supply, biodiversity, food and biomass, clean air supply and humidity control, energy, carbon storage and sequestration, and flood control. For too long we have disregarded these natural systems. Source: Graph supplied by the author

creating a zero-food-miles fish and vegetable supply chain on residents' doorsteps. Recent research concluded that a 50 sqm farm could provide 100 people with abundant fish and greens at low-to-no carbon emissions; in addition, surplus fish and vegetables could be sold to neighbours or used as fertiliser.

Understandably, all of these essential services cannot be valueless or priceless, but also have a significant value in monetary, financial terms. For example, a recent report calculated that street trees in California provide over US$1 billion per year in ecosystem services, through atmospheric regulation and flood prevention; and Mexico's mangrove forests provide an annual US$70 billion to the economy through storm protection, fisheries support and ecotourism (TEEB for Business Coalition 2013; Rizvi et al. 2015). The study calculated for the first time in monetary terms the financial risk from unpriced natural capital inputs to production, across business sectors at a regional level. By using an environmentally extended input-output model (EEIO), it also estimated, holistically and at a high level, how these may flow through global supply chains to producers of consumer goods. Interestingly, the study demonstrated that some business activities do not generate sufficient profit to cover their natural resource use and pollution costs (e.g. coal mining activities continuously ignore indirect costs to health) (Shanahan et al. 2015).

There is a real economy from natural capital that we are not discovering, or accounting for. We are getting the benefits but not recording the value. However, if natural capital were be lost we would feel it immediately, not least in economic terms. An accurate cost-benefit analysis is needed to find out what the real cost is of not doing the things we need to do for sustainability? Investment can then be made wisely.

Revaluing Parks and Green Spaces is a study published in 2018 that measures the economic and well-being value of parks and green spaces in UK cities to individuals. The research was conducted in line with HM Treasury's best practice in valuing non-market goods, and it provides a robust economic valuation of parks and green spaces in the UK as well as valuing improvements in health and well-being associated with their frequent use. It is the first study on parks and green spaces to apply welfare weighting methodology allowing for more informed evidence-based policy decisions. The study by UK charity Fields in Trust estimates that the country's parks and green spaces save the UK Government more than £111 million (US$200 million) in visits to the doctor each year (Fields in Trust 2018).

At the individual level, the study found that the Total Economic Value of using parks and green spaces breaks down annually to £30.24 of benefits per person. In addition, the *wellbeing value* associated with the frequent use of local parks and green spaces is estimated to be worth an incredible £34.2 billion (US$62.23 billion) per year to the UK adult population as a whole (see the research here: www.fieldsintrust.org/research). These findings are compelling figures to consider when discussing the business case for governments and stakeholders investing in more urban green spaces.

Giving 'ecosystem services' a monetary value allows for new measures of progress, which are not measured by simplistic GDP growth or other common economic measures. Based on these concepts, 'environmental justice' has emerged as a new term, meaning a focus on the fair distribution of the environmental benefits and burdens, increasingly informing environmental policy. Ideally, every person on the globe should 'enjoy the same equal access to a healthy environment in which to live, learn and work' (U.S. EPA 2012).

It is essential that every urban regeneration project comes with new public green space, small gardens and parks in a wide range of sizes. There are, of course, very different conceptions of what an urban park might be. For instance, Hyde Park in London has been open to the public since 1635 and demonstrates the value of a large (240 hectare in size) park in the city. Frederick Law Olmsted who designed New York's Central Park in the 1860s, conceived it as a large urban park (340 hectare in size) and a place to escape from the city, as a place in contrast to the surrounding city. Olmsted was committed to egalitarian ideals and believed that the common green space must always be equally accessible to all citizens, and defended against private encroachment. This principle is now fundamental to the idea of a 'public park', but was not assumed as necessary back then. Over a hundred years later, Bernard Tschumi, who designed *Parc de la Villette* in Paris (1982), viewed the park as a continuation of the city, with irregular non-hierarchical pathways that lead to nowhere in particular. Today, a public park for the twenty-first century is seen as a vital space for cooling cities, cross-cultural neighbourhood contact and social encounters, and as a spatial connector in an increasingly digital and segregated city.

We need more greenery and gardens in our cities, green roofs (planted areas combined with white-coloured roofscapes) and water features, like ponds and small lakes. Merging nature and food supply with the urban, the *Urban Manifesto* proposes an ecological network with a value system based on an economy of prosperity (not turnover) that also values our natural capital, so we can be citizens, not just merely consumers (Figs. 2.10 and 2.11).

Figs. 2.10 and 2.11 Vegetation and greenery keeps city temperatures cooler during summer, reducing the urban heat island effect. Special cameras reveal urban heat islands. Source: Graph and image supplied by the author. The informal green spaces of university campuses contribute positively to the city. Source: Image supplied by the author

References

Alberti, M., & Marzluff, J. (2004). Ecological Resilience in Urban Ecosystems: Linking Urban Patterns to Human and Ecological Functions. *Urban Ecosystems, 7*, 241–265.

BBC News. (2018). *UK's Most Polluted Towns and Cities Revealed.* Online News, 4 March 2018, Updated 4 May 2018. Retrieved July 10, 2018, from https://www.bbc.co.uk/news/health-43964341.

Benyus, J. (2002). *Biomimicry-Innovation Inspired by Nature.* New York: Harper Perennial.

Carson, R. (1962). *Silent Spring.* London and New York: Penguin Modern Classic.

Csikszentmihalyi, M. (1997). *Creativity. The Psychology of Discovery and Invention.* New York and London: Harper Perennial.

Ellen MacArthur Foundation. (2017). *The Circular Economy. A Wealth of Flows* (2nd ed.). Retrieved July 10, 2018, from https://www.ellenmacarthurfoundation.org/publications/the-circular-economy-a-wealth-of-flows-2nd-edition.

European Union Commission. (2017). *Nature-Based Solutions: Innovating with Nature.* Brussels: European Commission. Retrieved July 10, 2018, from https://ec.europa.eu/research/environment/index.cfm?pg=nbs.

European Union Commission, DG Research and Innovation. (2015). *Towards an EU Research and Innovate Policy Agenda for Nature-Based Solutions and Re-naturing Cities*; Final report of the Horizon 2020 expert group on 'Nature-based solutions and re-naturing cities', European Commission, Brussels, report available online; 70.

Fairchild, T. (1722). *The City Gardener.* London: T. Woodward.

Falk, N. (2018). Smarter Urbanisation and Capital Values. *Here & Now, 11*, 8–10, AoU, London.

Fields in Trust. (2018). *Revaluing Parks and Green Spaces.* Study published in 2018, UK. Retrieved July 10, 2018, from www.fieldsintrust.org/research.

Girardet, H. (2008). *Cities, People, Planet: Urban Development and Climate Change* (2nd ed.). London: John Wiley & Sons.

Hawken, P., Lovins, A., & Lovins, H. (1999). *Natural Capitalism. Creating the Next Industrial Revolution.* New York: Little Brown and Company.

Howard, E. (1902). *Garden Cities of To-Morrow.* London: Faber & Faber.

Kabisch, N., Frantzeskaki, N., Pauleit, S., Naumann, S., Davis, M., Artmann, M., et al. (2016). Nature-Based Solutions to Climate Change Mitigation and Adaptation in Urban Areas: Perspectives on Indicators, Knowledge Gaps, Barriers, and Opportunities for Action. *Ecology and Society, 21*(2), 39.

Kellert, S. R. (2011, movie). Biophilic Design. The Architecture of Life, Burlington, USA: Tamarack Media.

Latour, B. (2015). *Face à Gaïa: Huit conférences sur le Nouveau Régime Climatique.* Paris: Éditions La Découverte.

Lehmann, S. (2015). Urban Microclimates: Mitigating Urban Heat Stress. In S. Lehmann (Ed.), *Low Carbon Cities: Transforming Urban Systems* (p. 251). London: Routledge.

Lennon, M., & Scott, M. (2014). Delivering Ecosystems Services Via Spatial Planning: Reviewing the Possibilities and Implications of a Green Infrastructure Approach. *Town Planning Review, 85*(5), 563–587.

Lovelock, J. E. (1979). *Gaia, a New Look at Life on Earth*. Oxford: Oxford University Press.

Maes, J., & Jacobs, S. (2015). Nature-Based Solutions for Europe's Sustainable Development. *Conservation Letters*.

McDonough, W., & Braungart, M. (2002). *Cradle to Cradle: Remaking the Way We Make Things* (1st ed.). New York, NY: North Point Press.

McHarg, I. (1969). *Design with Nature*. New York: Doubleday/Natural History Press; Philadelphia: Falcon Press.

Meadows, D., Meadows, D. L., Randers, J., & Behrens, W. W. (1972). *The Limits to Growth: A Report for the Club of Rome's Project on the Predicament of Mankind*. New York, NY: Universe Books (1971 Report/1972 Book).

Meerow, S., Newell, J. P., & Stults, M. (2016). Defining Urban Resilience. A Review. *Landscape and Urban Planning, 147*, 38–49. https://doi.org/10.1016/j.landurbplan.2015.11.011.

MIT Senseable City Lab. (2018). *Treepedia*. Developed in collaboration with WEF; Cambridge MA, USA. Retrieved August 5, 2018, from http://senseable.mit.edu/treepedia.

Mitchell, T., & Harris, K. (2012). *Resilience: A Risk Management Approach*. Background Note ODI. London: Overseas Development Institute.

Morton, T. (2007). *Ecology Without Nature. Rethinking Environmental Aesthetics*. Cambridge, MA: Harvard University Press.

Neves, J., & Francke, I. (2012). Creative Product Design Using Biomimetics. *Design and Nature VI: Comparing Design in Nature with Science and Engineering, 4*, 149.

Register, R. (1987). *Eco-City Berkeley: Building Cities for a Healthy Future*. Boston: North Atlantic Books.

Rich, N. (2018). Losing Earth: The Decade We Almost Stopped Climate Change. *New York Times*, August 1. New York. Retrieved August 10, 2018, from https://www.nytimes.com/interactive/2018/08/01/magazine/climate-change-losing-earth.html.

Rizvi, A. R., Baig, S., & Verdone, M. (2015). *Ecosystems Based Adaptation: Knowledge Gaps in Making an Economic Case for Investing in Nature Based Solutions for Climate Change*. Gland, Switzerland: IUCN 48.

Sailor, D. J. (2014). A Holistic View of the Effects of Urban Heat Island Mitigation. In S. Lehmann (Ed.), *Low Carbon Cities: Transforming Urban Systems* (pp. 270–281). London: Routledge.

Shanahan, D. F., Lin, B. B., Bush, R., Gaston, K. J., Dean, J. H., Barber, E., et al. (2015). Toward Improved Public Health Outcomes from Urban Nature. *American Journal of Public Health, 105*(3), 470–477.

Tansley, A. G. (1935). The Use and Abuse of Vegetational Terms and Concepts. *Ecology, 16*(3), 284–307.

TEEB for Business Coalition. (2013). *Natural Capital at Risk*. Retrieved July 10, 2018, from https://www.trucost.com/publication/natural-capital-risk-top-100-externalities-business/.

The World Forum on Natural Capital. (2018). *What Is Natural Capital?* Retrieved July 10, 2018, from https://naturalcapitalforum.com/about/.

U.S. EPA. (2012). *Environmental Justice*. Policy by the EPA, Washington, DC. Retrieved July 10, 2018, from https://www.epa.gov/environmentaljustice.

University of Leicester. (2015). *State of Our Countryside: Land-Use Map of the UK*. Retrieved August 10, 2018, from https://www2.le.ac.uk/offices/press/press-releases/2015/june/state-of-our-countryside-land-use-map-of-the-united-kingdom-reveals-large-scale-changes-in-environment.

Watts, J. (2018). Domino-Effect of Climate Events Could Move Earth into a 'Hothouse' State. *The Guardian*, August 6. London. Retrieved August 10, 2018, from https://www.theguardian.com/environment/2018/aug/06/domino-effect-of-climate-events-could-push-earth-into-a-hothouse-state.

Wilson, E. O. (1984). *The Biophilia Hypothesis*. New York: Island Press.

World Health Organization (WHO). (2014). *Healthy Cities. Promoting Health and Equity*. Copenhagen. Retrieved July 10, 2018, from http://www.euro.who.int/en/health-topics/environment-and-health/urban-health/who-european-healthy-cities-network/healthy-cities-vision.

3

Understanding the Benefits of Urban Density

A denser and more compact city increases efficiencies in urban infrastructure and services through shorter distribution networks. Higher density cities encourage reduced transit through shorter trip lengths, since most amenities and public transport are more closely located. Can we reverse the impact of urban sprawl?

Urban sprawl has resulted in underutilisation of land and a car-dependent society, where the distinction between city centre and city edge has become diffuse. Today, architects can easily visualise alternative urban scenarios, forecast future demand and simulate the benefits of various density types to better inform policies and decision-making.

How can we improve our densification without having a negative impact on the neighbourhood? What are the smart new densification models for making an existing city more compact and mixed-use while respecting its built heritage?

Quantifying Urban Density Towards a More Sustainable City Form

Cities around the world are facing an ever-increasing variety of challenges to achieve sustainable urbanisation. The issue of *urban density* is closely connected to how our cities should evolve and perform in future. Urban density is a term used

© The Author(s) 2019
S. Lehmann, *Urban Regeneration*, https://doi.org/10.1007/978-3-030-04711-5_3

in urban planning and architecture to refer to the mathematical number of people inhabiting a given urbanised area, and the amount of floor area that has been built on a defined site. It is an important factor in understanding how urban development functions, and architects worldwide are searching for ideal density models for tomorrow's sustainable cities. Density and compactness are two closely related but different criteria, relevant for the transformation of cities to become more resilient to climate change. While a high degree of compactness is usually desirable, too much density can be detrimental to liveability, health and social well-being. More compact and interconnected cities are advantageous as these will help in curbing urban sprawl, but a consolidated urban form requires urban infill at densities that support compact self-reliant districts and mixed-use neighbourhoods. The social dimension of such density increase is likely to be a future challenge and face increased community resistance (e.g. in Switzerland, the average realisation time for a building has risen to eight years). Change and increase of density frequently meets community resistance, and public hearings about city developments can often be hostile. Today, density is one of the key issues in planning that can regularly create all kinds of misunderstandings and tension; it is an essential driver of our urban futures.

Defining Urban Density

In her book *The Death and Life of Great American Cities*, Jane Jacobs identified density as one of the four key ingredients for thriving and diverse cities. She wrote that in order for cities to work, 'there must be a sufficiently dense concentration of people, for whatever purposes they may be there' (1961, 36). Medium to high density living is acceptable as long as these developments also provide for a number of requirements, such as an increase in good quality green space within easy walking distance in the same neighbourhood. What is needed is a formula and framework for high-quality urban density and more compact and interconnected cities. Consolidated urban form is achieved through urban infill at densities that lead to compact, self-reliant and mixed use neighbourhoods. We use the term 'density' to describe the average number of people, households, floor space, or housing units on one unit of land, usually expressed in dwellings per hectare (Density Atlas 2011; OECD 2017).

There are different ways of mathematically measuring the density of urban areas, and these measures are a good way to describe density:

- floor area ratio: the total floor area of buildings divided by the land area of the plot upon which the buildings are built (the development plot ratio, used as a measure of the density of the site being developed); the ratio is generated by dividing the building area by the site area;
- residential density: the number of dwelling units in any given area (e.g. per hectare);
- population density: the number of persons living in any given area (e.g. per square kilometre).

The plot ratio (also called floor area ratio, FAR; or floor space ratio, FSR) describes the ratio of a building's total floor area (gross floor area) divided by the size of the site (piece of land or plot) upon which it is built. The term refers to limits imposed on such a ratio—for example, to the maximum allowable ratio. For instance, a FAR of 3.0 indicates that the total floor area of a building is three times the gross area of the plot on which it is built, as would be found in a multiple-story building. The allowable plot area has a major impact on the value of the land, as higher allowable plot areas yield a higher land value (see Figs. 3.1 and 3.4).

Using such zoning regulations, municipalities have found it unnecessary to include height limitations for buildings when applying maximum floor area ratio calculations. The FAR is commonly and successfully used in zoning regulations and planning guidelines to limit the amount of construction on a specific site or in a certain area. For example, if the relevant zoning ordinance permits construction on a site, and if construction must adhere to a 0.10 FAR, then the total area of all floors in all buildings constructed on the parcel must be no more than one-tenth of the area of the parcel itself.

An architect can plan for either a single-storey building consuming the entire allowable area in one floor, or a multi-storey building which must consequently result in a smaller footprint than would a single-storey building of the same total floor area. However, numerous urban planners have criticised the use of FAR regulation and argued that abdicating purely to floor area ratios (i.e. market forces) is the opposite of aiming for enhancing a community or neighbourhood and for diversity of ownership, as it is a poor predictor of physical urban form. Instead of pure FAR one could use the traditional design standards: building height, setbacks, or build-to lines rules; these would also enable planners to make reasonably accurate predictions, recognise violations, feel secure in investment decisions and are more likely to deliver a better outcome in terms of urban form (Batty and Longley 1994; Frey 1999).

Urban population densities can vary widely from city to city. Asian cities have some of the highest densities (frequently reaching over 10,000 people per square kilometre, and sometimes even over 20,000 people, such as in Mumbai or Hong Kong, where a large proportion of the buildings are high rise apartment towers). The historical European and UK cities have lower densities and are based on the European compact perimeter block model, with densities in the range of 3000 to 8000 people per square kilometre. Population densities in the range of 5000 to 10,000 people per square kilometre are common for cities of high liveability, such as Vienna or Copenhagen. In the United States, Canada and Australia, urban population densities are usually much lower, at around 1000 to 3000 people per square kilometre; Boston and New York are exemptions and have some of the highest urban densities of all US cities (Boston: 5344/sqkm; New York: 10,831/sqkm) (Lehmann 2010). Hence, there are three clearly identifiable city typologies that have their own characteristics, density profiles, and historical evolution (Figs. 3.1, 3.2, 3.3, 3.4, and 3.5):

- the European and UK compact and polycentric mid-rise city with the traditional perimeter block or rows of terrace houses (examples are London, Barcelona, Berlin, or Athens): 3000 to 8000 people per square kilometre;
- the Asian high rise city with distribution of individual towers (such as Shanghai, Beijing, Tokyo, and Bangkok): often around 10,000 to 12,000 people per square kilometre;
- the North American and Australian low rise and low density city typology with an urban downtown core surrounded by extensive car-dependent urban sprawl (for example, Las Vegas, Phoenix, Melbourne and Perth): urban density at only 1000 to 3000 people per square kilometre.

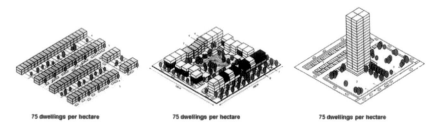

75 dwellings per hectare   75 dwellings per hectare   75 dwellings per hectare

Fig. 3.1 Diagram illustrating how the same density and number of dwellings on a site can be arranged in different ways, with the same plot ratio: as rows of terrace houses, as perimeter block, or in one single high-rise tower. Source: Graph supplied by the author

Figs. 3.2 and 3.3 A typical British housing block from the late nineteenth century; these are very popular for their large windows and high quality of living spaces. Source: Photo supplied by the author. Typical Georgian brick house in Salisbury. Source: Photo supplied by the author

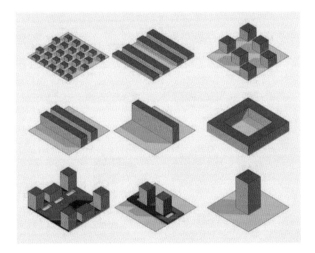

Fig. 3.4 Illustration of different density scenarios. Source: Graph supplied by the author

A high density city is therefore a city that has high average population density, high density of mixed-use built form, high density sub-centres, and reasonably high density forms of housing. Many researchers have argued that a denser, more compact city is a more sustainable city (Hall 1988; Jenks et al. 1996; Hall and Pfeiffer 2000). Susan Roaf noted that "high density (not high-rise) is probably the

Fig. 3.5 Diagram of different infill solutions to increase density.
Source: Graph supplied by the author

inevitable urban future" (2008, p. 33). Today, most experts agree that compact living is sustainable living. As an important benchmark for minimum densities of new sustainable developments, the literature gives the figure of a minimum of 70 dwellings (homes) per hectare, but densities should preferably be closer to 100 to 120 dwellings per hectare, especially along transport corridors, to support the integration of public transport, walking and cycling to key facilities, and on-site energy generation (Lehmann and Xie 2015).

Denser neighbourhoods have usually a lower carbon footprint per resident; in the UK there are helpful documents on this fact provided by CABE, the RIBA and the AoU. Lower density forces the residents to drive more, and there can also be great cultural benefits from higher densities. While a more compact city is usually more sustainable, expanding the city footprint farther and farther out into critical habitat areas, and in doing so losing precious agricultural land and green space is now seen as environmentally unacceptable. Cities like Portland (Oregon, USA) have achieved good experiences by establishing an effective urban growth boundary that curbed its sprawl since the 1970s. Recent research shows that Portland's compact city design has reduced the average car use by as much as 2000 kilometres per person per annum.

Planning can be understood as the generator of the city's urban code... the script for its development, while architecture focuses rather on the city's form, its physical and social manifestation.
—David Chipperfeld

Defining Density with Regard to the Compact City

Richard Rogers wrote in 1999 that 'the only sustainable form of development is the compact city' (The Urban Task Force and Rogers 1999). There has been plenty of evidence that more compact cities with higher densities encourage the use of public transport and bicycles, support closer amenities, increase efficiencies of infrastructure and land use, conserve valuable land resources at the fringe, and are likely to reduce the carbon emissions of urban dwellers (Hall 1988; Roaf 2008; Jenks et al. 1996; Lehmann 2005; Farr 2007; Toderian 2012). We should not be confused by the different denominations that have emerged to describe the 'compact city', which is sometimes also called green urbanism, sustainable urbanism, ecological urbanism, among others—it all means the same thing (Lehmann 2019).

So, what exactly is a *compact city*? A compact city is a mixed use spatial urban form characterised by a 'compactness', which defines a relatively dense urban area linked by easy access to public transport systems and designed to have minimal environmental impact by supporting walking and cycling (while low density suburbs are usually incapable of supporting walking, cycling, or any public transport due to lack of people). The compact city with four- to eight-storey urban perimeter blocks and shorter block length represents the optimum use of space (Lehmann 2014c, 2017). However, the compact city concept is still controversial and there is no single model or formula that can be replicated, as all cities and sites are different.

Development patterns with traditional urban characteristics usually have shorter block lengths with a network system of highly connected thoroughfares, local tree-lined streets and residential alleys. Vehicle-dominated contexts have larger, longer blocks, less street connectivity and usually no alleys; this pattern of longer blocks makes walking distances longer and, therefore, it is likely that fewer people will walk between destinations (see Fig. 3.8).

The benefits of urban density are often best realised when economies of scale are leveraged. The dense and compact city also increases efficiencies in urban infrastructure and services through shorter distribution networks. Higher density cities encourage reduced transit through shorter trip lengths, since most amenities and public transport are located closer together. Today, architects can easily visualise alternative density scenarios, simulate the benefits of various density types and inform policies and decision-making (Johnson 2017). Churchman (1999) defines compact city policies as policies that aim to intensify urban land use through a combination of higher residential density and centralisation, mixed land use, and limits on development outside of a clearly designated area (e.g. an urban growth boundary). Jenks, Burton and Williams (1996) outline three aspects of the compact city: it is high density, mixed use, and intensified. Urbanist Peter Rowe (2015) defines 'urban intensity' through a formula with four factors: *Urban intensity = Density + Diversity + Connectedness + Compactness.*

Architects use densification as a means of strengthening the community. However, making neighbourhoods more compact and dense always needs careful consideration and a process of optimisation to balance potential adverse effects. A recent survey in Bristol, accompanied by extensive consultation (2018), the city found in regard to people's attitude to higher densities that most residents were strongly of the opinion that new building heights should reflect the prevailing building height of those around it; while around 50 percent of the respondents agreed that new buildings should be allowed to be modestly higher than those around it. Support for the Bristol locations proposed for higher density development ranged from 24 percent (local and district centres) to 58 percent (on large vacant sites), with areas close to existing and proposed transport hubs receiving the second and third highest level of support (52 percent). The majority of respondents supported the aspiration to optimise densities, by balancing the more efficient and effective use of land, with an aspiration for successful place-making, liveable homes and a positive response to context. It was agreed to identify 'Urban Living Focal Areas' in Bristol where high density could be tested.

Higher density is beneficial at appropriate locations, but not always in every case. All urban areas have their particular social, cultural, environmental and climatic conditions resulting in a complex urban microclimate, and density increases can affect urban wind speeds. The interplay between higher density and the increased risk of the urban heat island effect (which increases energy demand for cooling) must be properly observed and taken into consideration. Density directly influences the urban microclimate. Negative effects on the urban climate can be improved by increasing greenery and vegetation, and choosing materials and surfaces that minimise solar heat gain and increase the albedo effect (surface reflection).

In this regard, it is important to understand the interplay between higher density and he increased risk of Urban Heat Island effect (Sharifi and Lehmann 2014; Lehmann 2014a, b).

To minimise adverse negative effects from increased densities, densification strategies should be coupled with high quality urban design strategies, scenario testing, and real community participation, to avoid such unwanted effects as increased traffic congestion, over-shading, and loss of daylight or privacy. It appears that the conflicting demands always have to be balanced through good design solutions. Planners and architects need a better understanding of the impact of their design decisions on the overall performance of the urban system and should introduce urban greenery in any densified areas.

Living in apartment blocks is often the more sustainable solution, as urban perimeter blocks and residential towers share circulation systems, separating walls and roofs, therefore requiring fewer construction materials and less heating. In the United States and Australia, researchers have now collected and analysed the actual energy use data for a large number of residential units, and there is emerging evidence that living in inner city high-rise buildings is a less energy-intensive lifestyle—all other things being equal—than in equivalent low rise buildings in suburbs, despite the need for elevators in the higher blocks. This is mainly due to two aspects: most of the suburban houses are larger in size and very energy intensive because of air-conditioning and other energy consuming devices; the other reason is the need to commute by car to the workplace.

But when is a city getting too dense, and at what point is a neighbourhood facing the threat of getting overdeveloped? Each time we create a higher density, we require an optimisation process since higher densities can create new challenges for planners and designers: avoiding over-shading, overlooking, loss of daylight and loss of privacy demands clever design solutions. There are a number of other arguments against high density, which include the risk of increasing traffic congestion in the area and a potential increase in noise disturbance. We can also point to districts where densities were developed too high and the developments failed because the lack of natural air ventilation or daylight created unhealthy and unhygienic conditions. A well-known example of such over-densification was the extremely dense *Kowloon Walled City* in Hong Kong, which was demolished in 1992–1993 because of the many issues that arose out of its extreme hyper-density. It is estimated that over 50,000 people lived there in squeezed conditions in dark cramped flats, on a small parcel of land of only 2 hectares. While *Kowloon Walled City* was a functioning urban community, it wasn't a sustainable or healthy place to live (Figs. 3.6, 3.7, 3.8, 3.9, and 3.10).

Social Experiments in Housing and Density in the Post-war Period: Britain's Tower Blocks

From the 1950s to the 1970s, post-war Britain saw a dramatic increase in *tower block* construction. Thousands were built in a very short time and they are still present in many British cities; thousands of tower blocks are dotted throughout Britain's cities and remain controversial. The tower block estates were built on cheap greenfield land at the fringe of established towns and cities, often without access to public amenities, such as public transport and shops. Even today, town

Figs. 3.6 and 3.7 Regeneration and retention are the drivers at the development of Wickside in Hackney. Source: Courtesy of Ash Sakula Architects, London (Cany Ash)

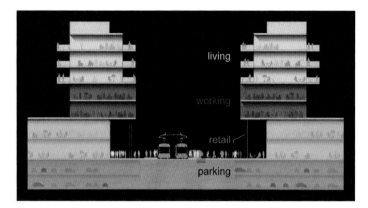

Fig. 3.8   Section through a mixed-use 7-storey urban block that combines living, working and retail with high-quality public space. Source: Graph by the author

Figs. 3.9 and 3.10   Housing blocks in the UK and in Paris. Source: Photos courtesy of Academy of Urbanism, London

planners are accused of having destroyed traditional neighbourhoods, tearing down streets of terraced houses with tight-knit communities in an attempt to modernise society (see Fig. 3.11).

The first residential tower block was constructed in Harlow, Essex in 1951. After an exhausting wartime period, authorities believed that replicating low-cost tower blocks in large numbers could provide a 'quick-fix' for housing problems, replacing unsanitary and crumbling nineteenth century dwellings. Local authorities and planners envisaged futuristic clusters of tower block estates, which would signify progress. The aesthetic of rough exposed concrete and expressed structural elements was applied to numerous new towns and tower blocks, which coined the term *New Brutalism* (Banham 1955).

Influenced by Le Corbusier's vision of high-rise architecture, including the concept of 'streets in the sky', local governments hoped that the way tower blocks were constructed (replicating the same typologies using industrial building techniques) would save money (Rosen 2003). Planners dreamt of reinventing society with new forms of urbanity. The optimistic vision of Swiss-French architect Le Corbusier, as expressed in his unbuilt project *Ville Contemporaine* (1922; and later by his built *Unite d'Habitation*), was that residential towers surrounded by public open space could provide for the same population density as the terraced housing and small private gardens they replaced, offering larger apartments and improved views. *Ville Contemporaine* was an unrealised utopian planned community of high-rise towers intended to house three million inhabitants, located in Paris where large areas of the old city would be destroyed to make space for this new district of tower blocks.

The new towns and tower blocks were a symbol for progress, and social and economic change. Initially, tower blocks were welcomed, but the estates soon deteriorated due to substandard construction methods and a lack of maintenance, with leaking roofs and structural decay, creating social problems and rising crime levels, turning the blocks into 'vertical slums' (Hanley 2007). In addition, tower blocks were unsuitable for families with children, as parents could not supervise them playing outside in front of the house. Today, the estates are a grim monument to Britain's failed post-war experiment in social housing (Dunleavy 1981). As a consequence of substandard-built housing, more social housing is currently getting demolished than built new, which is adding to the affordable housing crisis. Ultimately, the only option is to demolish the estates, yet dealing with decaying tower blocks will be expensive if councils choose to knock down entire blocks, finding somewhere else for their residents to live (Fig. 3.12).

Figs. 3.11 and 3.12   A typical cluster of 1960s British tower blocks. Source: Open source image. The visionary housing project 'Byker Wall' by Swedish architect Ralph Erskine (1970), a linear wall of 620 maisonettes built in Newcastle-upon-Tyne. Source: Photo supplied by the author

The Ongoing Density Debate

As urban populations and economies are expanding, and with increasing numbers of people joining the middle class (hence, earning and spending more), consumption, energy demand and waste generation are all rising. Due to our obsession with economic growth, the out-dated GDP-driven growth model, and excessive use of finite resources, global greenhouse gas emissions keep rising—despite all the efforts of the last 20 years to reduce them. It appears that there is a growing gap between the current urbanisation patterns and what would really be needed to shift to more sustainable urban futures (Jenks and Burgess 2000).

Numerous governments are now actively pursuing planning policies that encourage greater residential density and support a set of new densification measures to increase housing densities (e.g. in the UK, the Government is giving local councils increased powers to refuse development on the grounds of insufficient density).

The new Garden City at Ebbsfleet, Birmingham Interchange and Leeds South Bank (all projects presented in Chap. 5) will be composed of small blocks with pedestrian permeability and intensive activity focused around the new train station. It is an urban model of 4 to 6-storey blocks as transit-oriented development and with reasonable density, most likely to deliver future-proof new quarters.

One core challenge for cities in the future will be the tension between urban form, compactness, and liveability. The modern city is always about diversity, which includes varying urban densities for different neighbourhoods in different parts of the city (Howard 1902; Lynch 1960; Jacobs 1961; Rowe and Koetter 1978; Garreau 1992; Koolhaas and Mau 1995; Kostof 1999). This diversity of density types allows different demographic groups to choose how they would like to live at varying stages of their lives; for example, young professionals are now streaming back into the city and do not opt to live isolated out in the suburbs or far away from amenities and their workplace, expecting instead a more cosmopolitan lifestyle. Cities where residents don't need to drive much and efficient public transport is available have many advantages.

Hence, urban density and mixed usage are key factors in determining the sustainability of a neighbourhood and its urban liveability. Dense urban districts have a significant complexity about them and, clearly there is still a need for more research, comparative data, and an evidence base on the benefits and disadvantages of more dense and compact cities, which has frequently been noted by different scholars (Sennett 1974; Register 1987; Hall 1988; Breheney 1992; Jenks et al. 1996; Cuthbert 2006; Farr 2007; Girardet 2008; Lehmann 2010; Mostafavi and Doherty 2010; Beatley 2014).

Companies want to increasingly locate their headquarters in flexible loft spaces in central urban areas that give a feeling of cool urbanity, authenticity and vibrancy. This trend is getting stronger in all UK cities, and Manchester is at the forefront of it. For instance, NOMA is a mixed-use quarter within Manchester city centre, with a strong vision for its future and for 'curating a neighbourhood'. Balancing heritage, community and commercial interests, it is delivering a vibrant, responsibly-designed and authentic place for co-working, loft living and enjoyment. A 20-acre masterplan is creating new homes, offices, hotels, shops, restaurants and bars around vibrant urban spaces and public realm. NOMA champions the idea that places are better when people are involved in making them (see www.noma-manchester.com).

There is now a strong emphasis on regeneration projects, brownfield development and the introduction of minimum density targets for housing developments around transport hubs and along transport corridors (what is commonly known as transit-oriented development), and other strategies to create twenty-first century resilient regeneration. However, the link between urban density and sustainability remains a contested and often misunderstood subject of planning theory. One challenge cities face in their densification strategies is fierce resistance to higher densities from residents and community groups, as illustrated by the case of Vancouver's protesting neighbourhood groups. However, if done well, higher density does not decrease liveability (as can be seen in cities such as Singapore, Barcelona or London). Higher density living is acceptable as long as these developments also provide for easy access to new parks, gardens and urban greenery within walking distance of the neighbourhood; but a new park a drive away cannot be a substitute for new green space in the neighbourhood. It is with high quality urban design that we can alleviate negative perceptions of density at the metropolitan scale.

The choice of housing type directly influences the density of a neighbourhood. Density brings people together, and doing density well is as much about providing privacy as it is about civic life. Higher densities require new and better housing typologies, a wider range of housing models, and innovative design solutions that integrate urban greenery and high quality public space. Landscaping, green roofs, and the design of community spaces are important elements from the outset of each development (Lehmann 2010, pp. 708–719).

For the last 20 years, Hamburg's *HafenCity* was Europe's largest inner-city urban regeneration project. It is an extraordinary project and frequently used as a blueprint for the development typology of a European quarter on the waterfront. Like most industrial port cities, Hamburg had turned its back on its waterfront, the River Elbe and harbour, until the end of the twentieth century. Inspired by the possibilities demonstrated by the Spanish city of Bilbao, and after German reunification, Hamburg gained the confidence in the mid-1990s to regenerate this massive 157 hectares of port area and infrastructure. Plans for the HafenCity were developed to incorporate the inner-city waterfront into the Hamburg cityscape and also to expand and modernise port activities. By the time the masterplan will be complete (2025), over 2.4 million sqm floor area will be constructed, with 7500 residential units for over 15,000 residents, as well as 45,000 jobs, plus educational institutions (including a new university), with parks, plazas and promenades. The overall density of the project is considerable. The total investment will exceed Euro 13 billion. What sets it apart from other international urban waterside development projects is the area's central location, its innovative development process, fine-grained mix of uses and high standards of ecological sustainability. Rotterdam, Helsinki and other European port cities are now following the example of HafenCity.

The US-State of California has recently changed zoning laws for cities to allow higher-density developments. The California bill (2018) eliminates local restrictions on density, height and parking on properties that sit near rail stations and higher-frequency bus stops. It lifts planning rules for properties within half a mile of subway stations, light-railway platforms and stops where two high-frequency bus lines (those that run every 15 minutes during rush hour) intersect. In those areas, developers are now allowed to build apartments and condominium complexes of four to five stories; and five to eight stories for properties that are within a quarter-mile of railway stations.

With the UK Government committed to build 300,000 new homes a year by 2025, it is likely that there will be a further push towards higher densities and brownfield urban regeneration for a more effective use of the land available (before encroaching into protected Green Belt land) (Figs. 3.13, 3.14, 3.15, and 3.16).

Figs. 3.13 and 3.14 Inserting the new into the old: infill can happen in all sizes and does not need to be a large building: workshop for Alex Monroe.
Source: Courtesy of Luca Miserocchi and DSDHA Architects. The adaptive reuse of former industrial gasholders at King's Cross into a residential development.
Source: Photo courtesy of Peter Landers Photography

Figs. 3.15 and 3.16 The high quality of the public realm within the existing harbour structure at HafenCity Hamburg (designed by EMBT) offers a great diversity of spaces and reflects the general high standard of urbanity at this waterfront development project. Source: Photos supplied by the author. The new public space Granary Square at King's Cross in London. Source: Photos supplied by the author

Transforming North American Cities Through Strategic Density Increase?

All cities can transform their urban form to accommodate new configurations of programmes, connectivity and activities. For some cities, this process will take longer, while others can do it more quickly.

Let's look for instance at the case of North American cities, such as the city of Las Vegas. When living in the UK, I became interested in the density comparison of UK cities with US cities, and the question: What is it like to live in the driest desert city of North America, Las Vegas? How can an unsustainable condition be made resource-efficient and liveable? Comparing UK cities with US cities will help to better understand the urban qualities of cities in the United Kingdom.

The sprawling and urbanistically controversial city of Las Vegas is a particularly interesting case in its own right (Garreau 1992; Sorkin 1992; Hess 1993; Gandelsonas 1999; Inam 2016; De Salvatierra and Solana 2018). It is a geographically isolated city, and one of the fastest growing metropolitan areas in the US, including over 2 million inhabitants (according to UNLV population forecast, there will be an additional 835,000 people by 2035). Las Vegas region's first planning blueprint was recently launched with the hope to be able to better handle the predicted 45 percent population growth by 2045.

Different from most other cities in the world, Las Vegas has not been developed on the banks of a river or estuary. Located in the unforgivable climate of the Mojave Desert, where water scarcity and solar gain are key issues (solar radiation is so intense and plentiful, the whole city could be run just on solar power), and with weekend tourist numbers swelling the city's population up to 3 million, all of these people require water, energy, food and transport. Las Vegas gets less than five inches of rainfall in average a year—making it the driest city in the USA, where everything competes for what little water exists.

However instead of accepting the reality of 'Limits to Growth' (1972), Las Vegas is not known for resourcefulness, but for its display of boundless optimism in unrestrained growth. The city has a fragility and precariousness, but remains to a large degree in a state of denial about its environmental vulnerability. Scientists warn that in 50 years, due to global warming and soaring summer temperatures, Las Vegas and the American Southwest might become largely uninhabitable (Rich 2018).

The American city provides an interesting case to examine, because it is largely built by private investment (*the Strip* is a good example for this) and as a consequence, public policy is heavily shaped by private profit motives and initiatives, one of the reasons why the benefits of urban projects are unevenly distributed (Inam 2016). This means that projects concerning affordable housing, environmental measures or infrastructure for public transport are not always funded. Most of the city, apart from the Strip, is not pedestrian-friendly, and the windowless casinos along the Strip are designed with the aim to keep people inside.

Compared to the UK or Europe, the United States is always much harsher in its economic realities, leaving the complex urban issues to private developers rather than to experienced city planners with the civic good on mind. Throughout the twentieth century, the availability of cheap gasoline created the suburban construction era, but when petrol became more expensive it was no longer a good idea. Nevertheless, everybody drives in Las Vegas, nobody seems to walk within the residential neighbourhoods as these are mono-functional (not mixed-use), car-dependent (not walkable) and sprawling (not compact enough). Urban infill is a new concept in Las Vegas. While it is obvious to most planners that the future of Las Vegas will depend on the acceptance of a strict growth boundary and smart densification methods to slowly increase the population density, the necessary change in mind-set towards more ecological behaviour has not yet happened. On the other hand, a growth boundary for all development is increasingly recognised as the only way to reduce the current car-dependency and to enable feasible public transport in the form of a bus rapid transit system.

Las Vegas is one of the most interesting places in the US to study because it is such an intense hub of human activity and a product of the automobile era that is on the cusp of change. Numerous good initiatives are on the way: despite its reputation for being extremely wasteful, Las Vegas actually reuses 93 percent of its water (2017). This has become a necessity of survival as water resources keep shrinking. Lake Mead was created by the Hoover Dam in 1935 and provides water for 25 million people in southern Nevada, southern California and Arizona. 90 percent of the water in Las Vegas comes from Lake Mead. However, since 2000, the water level of Lake Mead is shrinking and with it Las Vegas' water supply. Therefore, a whole-hearted move towards water recycling was a matter of survival and gives hope that further initiatives will follow.

50 years after 'Learning from Las Vegas' (Venturi et al. 1969/1972), the new urban vision for Las Vegas includes taking more advantage of the abundance of solar energy available most days all year round (so far a widely untapped resource).

Here, the Nexus could become a powerful vision of restricting fossil energy use in favour of an abundance in renewable (solar) energy supply, helping to envisage a future powered by 100 percent solar energy (Scheer 2006; Droege 2008). Studies are also on the way to examine the whole life-cycle of the city, its buildings and neighbourhoods, and rethink its urban systems, to ensure economic growth does not damage the sensitive desert ecosystem.

The *Strip* is not the only lesson to be learnt from Las Vegas. The sprawling suburbs that stretch outward into the Las Vegas Valley and Mojave Desert are evidence that there are 'real' people living in Las Vegas. However, most residents of Las Vegas are living in a parallel world to the 43 million tourists that embark every year onto the city and spend most of their time around the Strip and its entertainment programme. It is a city with little truly public space as most of it is privatised, commercialised and controlled 24/7: this is the 'quasi' public space of the casinos, hotels and entertainment venues. Most of the time, pedestrian circulation along the Strip leads to indoor passages within the casinos and resorts. The indoor pedestrian realm is much larger than the outdoor realm; it is the real sidewalk of Las Vegas (Atwood and Schwarz 2010).

The U.S. trend of public spaces and sidewalks becoming commercialised, internalised and guarded by private security has also arrived in UK cities; it is a dangerous one, as it will create areas that poorer residents are unable to enjoy. Studies have indicated that excessive control and CCTV is detrimental to the quality of public space, and the need to create inclusive public space for the economically marginalised. In our cities today, public space is under constant threat of losing its true 'public' characteristics.

For a long time, we have created monocultures instead of mixed-use neighbourhoods, and the city of Las Vegas is a good example of a global city based for too long on an out-dated urban development model that has come to an end. Las Vegas has a population density of only 4370 people per square mile (data: 2018), compare this to Manchester: the UK city of Manchester has a population density of over 11,500 people per square mile (three times higher than Las Vegas) and is just the 9th densest city in the United Kingdom.

The edge of the city encroaches and continues to sprawl into the vulnerable ecology of the Mojave Desert. The periphery, the edge where vulnerable wilderness meets encroaching suburban sprawl, reveals the all-too-real paradoxes of life in the desert. A more responsive approach will have to be developed that fits the sensitive fragile conditions of the desert's ecosystem. The city of Las Vegas has an unusually large number of gated communities, resort-style like housing clusters incorporating 58 golf courses and vast pool areas—with lush green grass, artificial waterways and tropical palm trees set against the waterless desert landscape. Around 70 percent of the Las Vegas population lives in these gated communities; these master planned estates are resort-style clusters of houses around landscapes of pools and golf courses, with vacant land in-between (see Fig. 3.18).

Since the 2008 financial crisis, Southern Nevada and Las Vegas has had the most over-heated and the hardest-hit residential and commercial real estate market in the US. Few cities were hit as hard as Las Vegas by the financial crisis and following recession. Nevada as a whole lost more jobs in relation to its workforce than any other state, with more than 70 percent of those losses in the Las Vegas region (in 2009, the unemployment rate hit a record 14.2 percent).

U.S. cities have a unique history and physical attributes that require tailored strategies to overcome the prevailing car-dominated culture. The recent trend to introduce light-railway systems in US cities is remarkable, as the lack of population densities frequently undermines the potential of rail interventions. In addition, the high cost of infrastructure and a privately dominated real estate market often push railway stations towards the edge of the city.

Though construction cranes once again rise above *Sin City*, Las Vegas is trying to build economic resilience and diversify its economy to move away from the sole reliance on hospitality and tourism (mostly low-paying hospitality jobs account for almost a third of the region's workforce). New growing industries range from medical care to professional sports and IT start-ups in big data industries. The cluster of medical office buildings and hospitals north of the Strip will make a significant contribution to the local economy. The University of Nevada's Medical Centre is at the core of the city's vision of its future, expected to add 8000 new jobs by 2030.

There are now serious plans for a new light-railway line that will connect the airport and UNLV campus with the Medical Centre in downtown, which is a good idea, as such, a public funded infrastructure project would result in immense private sector investment in the surrounding areas around the proposed light-rail stops. This has been the experience in other cities introducing light-railway, from Portland to Phoenix and Denver, where a development boom with mixed-use high-density projects followed the initial investment in public transport and public space.

More recently, Las Vegas Downtown has put itself on the map as an emerging start-up hub and innovation district, and in 2017, the first completely autonomous electric shuttle bus in the US was deployed on its public roadways. With new concepts of densification and infill arriving, Las Vegas will have to re-adjust its thinking about future housing: every year, over 10,000 new homes are built in Las Vegas, but what kind of housing is getting produced, at what densities, and in what location? Still today, these are frequently poorly insulated light-weight houses entirely dependent on their energy-hungry air-conditioning systems, there are no green roofs and there is a lack of strategic planning that takes passive design principles such as geometry and orientation into account. This kind of housing will always lead to an inefficient use of resources.

The Strip resembles the fake New Urbanist towns that feel like stepping into a set of *The Truman Show*. Can such contrived places be successful as urban models? The Strip's textureless surfaces make the big casinos along the entertainment street appear as one large over-scaled space where everything is blurred together, shouting for attention (what Robert Venturi called 'the decorated shed'). It is the lack of texture that Aaron Betsky calls 'walmartism', critiquing a built environment of boxes devoid of texture and urban complexity. The concept and value of urban complexity is central to many of the writings on cities (for instance, by Richard Sennett). The surfaces along the Strip are all smooth, flat and often shiny, and the graphics bold and colourful, adding to too much visual noise. The spatial differentiation along the Strip comes mainly from an arrangement of drop-off areas in front of hotels and casinos, rather than from a change in definition to create diverse functional areas. The obvious reason for all this screaming sameness is economics: texture is more expensive both to build and to maintain, while these are guided by design decisions that save costs in materials, assembly and cleaning.

All of this exemplifies why Las Vegas and the North American cities are such an interesting and urgent case for comparative research with UK cities and as urban living labs, again the subject of much exploration how unsustainable cities may best be transformed. How far will Las Vegans go to live in a place not intended for living and could their desires to do so, in the end, ever be sustainable?

50 years on, there is still so much to learn from Las Vegas! However, it also makes us re-appraise the European city model for all its diversity and the qualities it offers and which we take often for granted. Let us work hard so that our cities become more compact, walkable and mixed-use, countering urban sprawl (Figs. 3.17, 3.18, and 3.19).

100   S. Lehmann

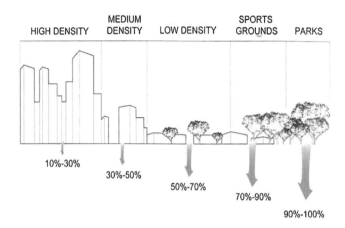

Fig. 3.17 As urban density increases and there are more non-penetrable surfaces, additional solutions are required to ensure that rainwater can recharge the groundwater. Source: Graph courtesy of Thomas Spiegelhalter

Fig. 3.18 Aerial photo of Las Vegas. In density North American cities are fundamentally different from cities in the UK. Las Vegas in Nevada is a fast-growing city of 2 million residents located in the Mojave Desert; in comparison, in 1970 Las Vegas only had 120,000 residents. Source: Open source image

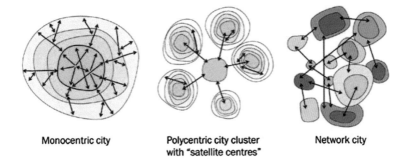

Monocentric city   Polycentric city cluster   Network city
with "satellite centres"

Fig. 3.19 The polycentric structure of a network city, where various downtown areas with higher density around transport nodes are inter-connected through a very efficient public transport system, is the most sustainable urban model for cities larger than 1 million people (Lehmann 2010). Source: Graph supplied by the author

A Proposed Framework for 'Quality Density'

Cases of recent higher density housing developments have enabled residents to live closer to their workplaces. Such intensification through urban infill at an appropriate density is a sustainable design strategy, as it avoids and counteracts the further dispersion and fragmentation of activity centres, and helps to reduce car dependency. Urban densities must remain within a sustainable range. If density is too low, it must be allowed to increase; and if it is too high, it must be allowed to decline, to arrive at the most appropriate 'quality density'. However, most of the time densities are too low in cities around the world and are in decline everywhere, so that there is now a concern among urban experts worldwide about declining densities in cities across the globe, a situation that is exacerbating urban challenges such as sprawl and traffic congestion.

It has frequently been suggested that quality density cannot always be planned or predicted; it depends on the socio-economic context. While every city is different, some guiding principles of ideal development with quality density have been identified (Pont and Haupt 2010; Bay and Lehmann 2017), which include increasing compactness and the integration of public transport, greenery and mixed usage. Policy-makers now have to take decisive, forward-looking steps in urban planning and decision making on density to create room for long-term physical development toward a sustainable city form. As a framework for quality density, the following six components have been identified as prerequisites for appropriate quality density of a compact city:

- A strong alignment of land use and mobility: the efficient public transport city;
- Proximity and 'nearness' to amenities: *the walkable city*;
- For 'city-regeneration', we need new buildings that provide a continuity of urban context, not objects in isolation: *the authentic city*;
- To keep cities cool, the integration of urban greenery and green roofs needs to go hand in hand with densification: *the green city*;
- High quality architectural and urban design by using design competitions, with more diversity and better examples of residential infill through four- to eight-storey projects: *the mixed-use city*;
- More innovative design solutions (including off-site manufactured homes) need to be developed to ensure there is no negative impact on neighbouring sites from densification, such as loss of privacy (overlooking) or loss of daylight (over-shading): *the city of innovative housing solutions.*

Groups of buildings that form quarters are of great interest, as these can support the public realm, perform and interact, with a density of mixed functions, and connect with each other. Very dense high-rise cities are not necessarily the best option. Medium density, compact infill developments of four- to eight-storey perimeter blocks are the much-preferred option and a very useful model, as the perimeter block combines a number of benefits, such as:

- Smaller building envelopes (good ratio between the area of the facade and the enclosed volume), using less land and reducing heat gain in summer and heat loss in winter;
- Less material used, therefore lower construction impact and reduced embodied energy;
- Reduced energy consumption due to shared walls, efficient circulation and roofs.

Learning to Live in More Compact and Denser Communities

In a world where property prices are rising and homes are increasingly unaffordable, 'infill' also means to build extra homes in mews or the backyards of single-family houses that will help to ease the housing crisis, reduce gentrification and add value to existing properties. It is estimated that another one million small units could be added immediately in UK cities, where gap sites are available at numerous properties in the repetitive suburban landscape, just by tapping into this unused resource and site capacity, without the need to find and buy any new site. We need new ideas for housing, and these small-scale lightweight insertions with their tight and compact plans could just be the solution for densification in an intelligent way. Thoughtful, easily replicable solutions with separate access to increasing density on the under-used spaces in back-gardens: this could include micro-housing types or co-housing clusters, added in the rear gardens of existing houses as lightweight modular additions (as kit-of-parts).

If even a fraction of the cities' backyards were repurposed and infilled with additional housing, it could go a long way toward solving the affordable housing crisis. Building codes will need to be changed to allow for and facilitate such densification through small backyard units. As rents keep rising, driven by the housing shortage, we need to activate new solutions and make it easier to build accessory dwellings as backyard homes that could allow for multi-generational living (e.g. 'granny flats' above the garage) or prefabricated modular garden studios for renting. However, facilitating this infill process will require a change in mind-set to accept denser communities, reduce the large fees to connect backyard homes to utilities, remove absurd parking requirements in neighbourhoods near public transport, and councils supporting difficult negotiations with neighbours. While it will contribute to easing the pressure, we should not expect backyard infill housing to solve the housing crisis on its own; this will require a mix of initiatives where large apartment buildings and other urban development will fill most of the gap (see Fig. 3.5).

Infill is very much like urban dentistry, where you are inserting an implant into a street. Replacing an earlier implant, for such is the nature of cities.
—**Hugh Pearman**

While urban density is extremely relevant, it is of course not the only determining factor for urban form. In fact, urban developments are rarely the pure result of design considerations; rather they are shaped by economic forces, the evolution of policies, and a range of invisible forces such as land use regulations, codes for floor space ratios, and economic power structures. There is always a multiplicity of complex forces and flows that form a city, and the forces that are shaping the city are not limited to the physical spectrum only. Long-term trends in economies, energy supply and demand, geopolitical shifts, and social change are all additional drivers of urban development.

How densely we plan our cities determines how efficiently we use vital resources, which directly affects the quality of life of urban citizens. Growth boundaries are an effective tool to contain the footprint of cities, leading to more infill in already built-up areas to avoid urban sprawl, as cities cannot continue to expand their boundaries simply due to population increases. For a long time, the high infrastructure costs and inefficiencies caused by urban sprawl have somehow been accepted on the wrongful assumption that sprawl would provide affordable housing. Now planners will need to increase the suburbs' densities and transform out-dated urban values into acceptance of higher densities and more public transport.

There is definitely a limit to urban density. Arguing for a new ethics of the urban, we can say that the traditional urbanism of the UK or European city (such as in Manchester or Liverpool, as well as in Barcelona, Paris, Berlin or Athens) is also ecological urbanism (Lehmann 2010). Urban density should be embraced more strategically as the answer to a number of challenges facing today's urban developments. It is time to begin thinking about our cities in a completely new way (Figs. 3.20 and 3.21).

Figs. 3.20 and 3.21   As densities increase, it is important to enhance open public space and re-green of cities. Zeche Zollverein industrial landscape in Essen. Source: Photo supplied by the author. A new public walkway and urban void in Ripoll, Spain. Source: Photo supplied by the author

References

Atwood, C., & Schwarz, D. M. (2010). *Learning in Las Vegas*. New Haven: Yale School of Architecture Publication.

Banham, R. (1955). The New Brutalism. *Architectural Review* (AR), December. London.

Batty, M., & Longley, P. (1994). *Fractal Cities: A Geometry of Form and Function*. London: Academic Press.

Bay, J. H. P., & Lehmann, S. (Eds.). (2017). *Growing Compact: Urban Form, Density and Sustainability*. London: Routledge.

Beatley, T. (2014). Imagining Biophilic Cities. In S. Lehmann (Ed.), *Low Carbon Cities*. London: Routledge.

Breheney, M. (Ed.). (1992). *Sustainable Development and Urban Form*. London: Pion.

Churchman, A. (1999). Disentangling the Concept of Density. *Journal of Planning Literature, 13*(4), 389–411. London: SAGE.

City of Bristol. (2018). *Urban Living SPD*. Report June 2018, City Design Group, Bristol, UK. Retrieved July 10, 2018, from https://bristol.citizenspace.com/growth-regeneration/urban-living/results/urbanliving-responsesreceivedduringconsultation-june2018.pdf.

Cuthbert, A. R. (2006). *The Form of Cities: Political Economy and Urban Design*. Oxford: Blackwell.

De Salvatierra, A., & Solana, S. (2018). On the Liminal Fertility Between the Sacred and Profane in the Sin City of Neon Lights. ACSA/COAM 2018 Proceedings, Madrid (presented paper); UNLV, Las Vegas.

Density Atlas. (2011). Planning Resource Developed by MIT Faculty. Available online.

Droege, P. (2008). *Urban Energy Transition: from Fossil Fuels to Renewable Power*. Oxford: Elsevier Books.

Dunleavy, P. (1981). *The Politics of Mass Housing in Britain, 1945–1975*. Oxford: Clarendon Press.

Erskine, R. (1970). Hidden Town, Project Text. Available Online.

Farr, D. (2007). *Sustainable Urbanism*. New York, NY: McGraw-Hill Publishers.

Frey, H. (1999). *Designing the City: Towards a More Sustainable Urban Form*. London: Spon Press, Taylor & Francis Group.

Gandelsonas, M. (1999). *X-Urbanism: Architecture and the American City*. New York: Princeton Architectural Press.

Garreau, J. (1992). *Edge City: Life on the New Frontier*. New York: Penguin Random House.

Girardet, H. (2008). *Cities, People, Planet: Urban Development and Climate Change*. London: Wiley.

Hall, P. (1988). *Cities of Tomorrow: An Intellectual History of Urban Planning and Design in the Twentieth Century*. Oxford and New York: Blackwell.

Hall, P., & Pfeiffer, U. (2000). *Urban Future 21: A Global Agenda for 21st-Century Cities*. New York, NY: Spon.

Hanley, L. (2007). *Estates: An Intimate History*. London: Granta Books.

Hess, A. (1993). *Viva Las Vegas: After-hours Architecture*. San Francisco: Chronicle Books.

Howard, E. (1898/1902/1965). *Garden Cities of Tomorrow*. London: Faber & Faber.

Inam, A. (2016). Unveiling Vegas: Urbanism at the Nexus of Private Profit and Public Policy. *Journal of Urbanism: International Research on Place-Making and Urban Sustainability, 9*(3), 216–236.

Jacobs, J. (1961). *The Death and Life of Great American Cities.* London/New York: Cape/ Random House.

Jenks, M., & Burgess, R. (Eds.). (2000). *Compact Cities. Sustainable Urban Forms for Developing Countries.* London: Spon Press.

Jenks, M., Burton, E., & Williams, K. (Eds.). (1996). *The Compact City: A Sustainable Urban Form?* London: Spon.

Johnson, C. (2017). Growing Sydney: Advocacy for Urban Density. In J. H. P. Bay & S. Lehmann (Eds.), *Growing Compact* (pp. 343–357). London and New York: Routledge.

Koolhaas, R., & Mau, B. (1995). *S, M, L, XL.* New York, NY: Monacelli Press.

Kostof, S. (1999). *The City Shaped: Urban Patterns and Meaning Through History* (2nd ed.). New York, NY: Thames & Hudson.

Lehmann, S. (2005). Towards a Sustainable City Centre: Integrating Ecologically Sustainable Development Principles into Urban Sprawl. *Journal of Green Building, 1*(3), 83–104.

Lehmann, S. (2010). *The Principles of Green Urbanism.* London: Routledge.

Lehmann, S. (2014a). Low Carbon Districts: Mitigating the Urban Heat Island with Green Roof Infrastructure. *City, Culture & Society, 5*(1). Elsevier (27 March 2014), pp. 1–8. https://doi.org/10.1016/j.ccs.2014.02.002.

Lehmann, S. (2014b). Green Districts and Carbon Engineering: Increasing Greenery, Reducing Heat Island Effects and Generating Energy. In S. Lehmann (Ed.), *Low Carbon Cities. Transforming Urban Systems* (pp. 191–209). London and New York: Routledge.

Lehmann, S. (2014c). *Low Carbon Cities: Transforming Urban Systems.* London: Routledge.

Lehmann, S. (2017). The Challenge of Transforming a Low-Density City into a Compact City. The Case of the City of Perth, Australia. In H. W. P. Bay & S. Lehmann (Eds.), *Growing Compact: Urban Form, Density and Sustainability* (pp. 69–93). London and New York: Routledge.

Lehmann, S. (2019). Urban Density. In A. Orum (Ed.), *Wiley-Blackwell Encyclopaedia of Urban and Regional Studies* (pp. 1–9). Hoboken, NJ: J. Wiley & Sons Publishing.

Lehmann, S., & Xie, H. T. (2015). A Green Urban Development Agenda for the Asia-Pacific, pp. 152–157. In *State of Asian and Pacific Cities 2015*. Report published by UN-HABITAT and UN-ESCAP, Nairobi/Bangkok. Available online.

Lynch, K. (1960). *Image of the City.* Cambridge, MA: MIT Press.

Mostafavi, M., & Doherty, G. (Eds.). (2010). *Ecological Urbanism.* Baden, Switzerland: Lars Mueller.

OECD. (2012). *Compact City Policies: A Comparative Assessment.* Report available online.

OECD. (2017). *Green Growth Studies.* Paris: OECD Publishing. Retrieved July 10, 2018, from http://www.oecd.org/greengrowth/.

Pont, M. Y., & Haupt, P. (2010). *Spacematrix: Space, Density and Urban Form.* Rotterdam: NAi Publishers.

Register, R. (1987). *Eco-City Berkeley: Building Cities for a Healthy Future*. Boston: North Atlantic Books.

Rich, N. (2018). Losing Earth: The Decade We Almost Stopped Climate Change. *New York Times*, August 1. New York. Retrieved August 10, 2018, from https://www.nytimes.com/interactive/2018/08/01/magazine/climate-change-losing-earth.html.

Roaf, S. (2008). The Sustainability of High Density. Population and the People. In E. Ng (Ed.). 2009. *Designing High-Density Cities for Social and Environmental Sustainability* (pp. 27–33). London: Earthscan.

Rosen, A. (2003). *The Transformation of British Life 1950–2000: A Social History*. Manchester: Manchester University Press.

Rowe, P. G. (2015). Urban Density as a Function of Four Factors. YouTube Video of Rowe's Presentation at the Centre for Liveable Cities, Singapore, September 2015. Retrieved October 25, 2017, from www.youtube.com/watch?v=IXahgHQEuMI.

Rowe, C., & Koetter, F. (1978). *Collage City*. Cambridge, MA: MIT Press.

Scheer, H. (2006). *Energy Autonomy*. London: Routledge.

Sennett, R. (1974). *The Fall of Public Man*. New York: Faber.

Sharifi, E., & Lehmann, S. (2014). Comparative Analysis of surface Urban Heat Island Effect of Rooftops and Streetscapes in Central Sydney. *Journal of Sustainable Development, 7*(3), 23–34. Canadian Center of Science and Education. https://doi.org/10.5539/jsd.v7n3p23.

Sorkin, M. (Ed.). (1992). *Variations on a Theme Park: The New American City and the End of Public Space*. New York: Hill & Wang.

The Urban Task Force, & Rogers, R. (1999). *Towards an Urban Renaissance* (Report, June 1999). London: UTF/DETR/E & FN Spon. Available online.

Toderian, B. (2012). Density Done Well. YouTube Video of Toderian's Presentation at the Vancouver Urban Forum 2012, June 2012. Retrieved October 25, 2017, from www.youtube.com/watch?v=eRk93Wgdv1g.

Venturi, R., Scott Brown, D., & Izenour, S. (1969/1972). *Learning from Las Vegas*. Cambridge, MA: MIT Press.

4

Activating the Food-Water-Energy Nexus

Resource challenges are particularly dominant in expanding cities and include inefficient infrastructural systems which can lead to energy black-outs, urban flooding, water leakages, lack of recycling or increased emissions and air pollution. The *Food-Water-Energy Nexus* is a new field of research that studies the interrelated complex system where food, water, energy and waste treatment (material flow) systems intersect (Gold and Bass 2010). It is likely that this new field will have significant impact on the future re-engineering of our cities.

Cities are where everything is integrated. This chapter, therefore, addresses the development of integrated infrastructure planning approaches as a tool for increased resource efficiency in regeneration projects and aims to link the circular economy discourse with the urban nexus approach. Informed planning for future urban regeneration and economic development requires a good understanding of this multitude of interdependencies within the food-water-energy nexus, towards a cross-sectorial urban ecosystem approach.

This chapter also introduces the *CRUNCH Urban Nexus* project along with some urban challenges that are likely to be encountered.

© The Author(s) 2019
S. Lehmann, *Urban Regeneration*, https://doi.org/10.1007/978-3-030-04711-5_4

What Is the Food-Water-Energy Nexus?

Some of the greatest challenges to urban development include: rising consumption levels, system inefficiencies (due to inadequate or underdeveloped infrastructure), severe shortages of affordable housing, dysfunctional land and housing markets, transportation and mobility challenges, socio-economic issues and environmental degradation. These impact urban resource efficiency and the sustainable management of natural resources. At the same time, these challenges put increased pressure on water supply and sanitation, energy supply and efficiency, waste recycling and resource recovery, land use and food security in particular. The interdependence of the various sectors points towards the urgency of better integrated systems and the advantages a circular economy approach could deliver, acknowledging this inter-connectedness between infrastructural systems (a challenge that was specifically highlighted by the UN at the Rio+20 outcomes as well as in the 2030 Agenda for Sustainable Development 2016).

What could the infrastructure of the future be? We are still building the infrastructure of the twentieth century with some small modifications. However, the infrastructure of tomorrow is likely to be fundamentally different, decentralised and more interconnected. For instance, the 5G-internet platform is necessary for autonomous transport and the *Internet-of-Things*, so this super-fast new internet platform will need to be part of tomorrow's infrastructure. But the new green infrastructure is also about innovative wastewater treatment technology, integrated PV-cells for solar power and water-saving hydroponic food systems.

This chapter explores the interconnectedness (and interdependencies) of the various 'siloed' sectors of food, water, energy, waste treatment (material flows), and transport. As action in one sector affects the others, a multi-sectoral and multi-jurisdictional approach is essential to ensure that the optimal combination of policies, programmes and financial instruments is put in place to inform planning and investment decisions that will enable sustainable economic growth (UN ESCAP 2011).

Typically, options for solving problems facing the food, water, energy or waste sectors are approached in isolation and in piece-meal planning, eg. exploring how to meet water needs whilst overlooking the implications for energy consumption, or setting targets to change land-use and ignoring knock-on impacts for agriculture. This 'silo' mind-set does not allow us to acknowledge important interconnections between these systems or explore the potential benefits or trade-offs.

The systems of food, water and energy intersect in various ways, for instance:

- Agriculture and land use affect energy and water; food production and land use practices impact water quality and runoff; some crops, plant residues and agricultural lands can be used for energy production.
- Water is required for energy and agriculture, from cooling of thermal power plants, hydro-power and bio-fuel production, to irrigation and food processing.
- Energy is required for water and agriculture, from extraction, transportation, treatment and disposal of water, to livestock production, fertilizer and energy for irrigating crops and transporting food to markets.

The environment's capacity to support human needs (eg. the ever rising demands for water, food and energy) is decreasing as a result of human actions, such as alteration to land cover and population growth—leading to escalating energy and food prices. As a consequence, the environment's ability to deliver the essential ecosystem services necessary to support the survival of future generations is being undermined (Folke 2006; IPCC 2015; Potschin et al. 2016).

Urbanisation is the catalyst for many of the challenges mentioned. The low-density growth of urban areas continues to convert (often in an uncoordinated manner) productive natural and agricultural land into urbanised areas (Arezki et al. 2015). The rising demand for more urban space and the desire for higher quality of life coincides with growing consumption levels, increasing vulnerability to climate change impacts and declining investment in public green space, all contributing to lower urban resilience. In addition, urban design, planning and management still happen along sectoral lines (in 'silos'), rather than as an integrated process, meaning municipalities have been unable to utilise the potential synergies across the Food-Water-Energy-Waste (FWEW) sectors or exploit the benefits of better integrated resource management (see: Figs. 4.1 and 4.2).

Cities, like dreams, are made of desires and fears, even if the thread of their discourse is secret, their rules are absurd, their perspectives deceitful, and everything conceals something else.—Italo Calvino

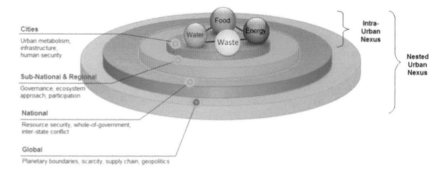

Fig. 4.1 Intra and nested perspectives of the Urban EWFW Nexus (Lehmann 2018a)

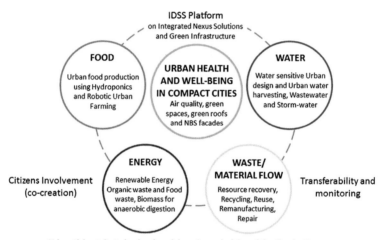

Fig. 4.2 Interconnecting infrastructures: the Urban Nexus thinking is central to health and well-being in cities. To holistically transform the urban systems, waste/material flows must be part of the approach (by the author 2018)

Introducing the *CRUNCH Urban Nexus* Project

The *CRUNCH Urban Nexus* project, initiated by 20 significant organisations from six countries, commenced in 2017 and is currently in its second phase (2018–2020). It was initiated by, and is supported by the author and the Cluster for Sustainable Cities, and aims to integrate resource management processes that increase the efficiency of natural resource use, to transform infrastructural systems and planning practice that will reduce CO_2 emissions and waste generation. The approach is based on the untapped interdependencies between the sectors (rather than understanding these in an isolated single-purpose, single-sector linear way). See the following web site for more information on CRUNCH: www.fwe-nexus.eu

The urban nexus approach enables a closer link between the principles of the circular economy and urban planning (EMF 2014/2017). The objective of the Nexus project is therefore to provide an informed framework for determining trade-offs and synergies to meet future demand for post-regeneration projects, increasing urban resilience and resource efficiency without compromising safeguards for environmental protection. The *Resource Nexus* has strong overlaps with the concept of the *Circular Economy*.

Why Is an Urban Nexus Necessary, and What Is It Aiming For?

When land is converted through the process of urbanisation, the landscape is intensely transformed and precipitation systems, hydrological cycles, the productivity of the ecosystem, energy balance and local climate are all disrupted and modified (Alberti 2005; Foley et al. 2011). While UK cities currently use merely 2 percent of land cover (Schneider et al. 2009: 182), resource availability constraints and climate change create challenges for the provision of healthy food, essential energy and clean water supply for a growing population.

The term Nexus refers to the need for integrated holistic approaches across the sectors (Bazilian et al. 2011). It describes the key interactions between parts of a system or systems. The Nexus is aiming to integrate resource management processes that increase the efficiency of natural resource use and infrastructural systems, transform planning practice and reduce CO_2 emissions and waste generation. The approach is based on the (currently) untapped inter-dependencies between the sectors and is estimated to deliver over 20 percent increase in resource efficiency, for instance, by looking holistically at the energy and water system as part of a multi-dimensional network of urban systems.

Urban experts agree that most of the current systems of food, water and energy provision, and waste treatment for material recovery are on an unsustainable course (Bringezu and Bleischwitz 2009), meaning that systemic change is required. Policy and decision makers are concerned that climate change impacts, an overuse of land and increasing inequality threaten our food, water and energy security and will place pressure on future cities globally. Moreover, with targets to cut greenhouse gas emissions, stakeholders from civil society, industry and government are looking for support and guidance for 'good' decision-making in urban design and development.

The aim of the *CRUNCH Nexus* project is to look holistically at activating the sectoral inter-linkages and principles of a resource-efficient city, by establishing a closer dialogue between national and local governments to identify and remove policy barriers and create new strong partnerships at the local level. It aims to enhance co-operation between different levels of government, municipal administrations (departments) and planning offices, city administrations and across city jurisdictions. In terms of better decision making, is developing an integrated decision support system (IDSS).

It is essential for the *CRUNCH Nexus* project to identify the policy barriers that are currently holding back the promotion of integrated resource management in cities and to work towards enabling factors and solutions to remove these barriers. The enabling factors for the Urban Nexus are illustrated in the following Figure (Fig. 4.3). Urban governance and community engagement play an important role in delivering food/water/energy supply security. The solution based approach aims to understand the risks, to better engage decision-makers and empower citizen participation, project partners and local leaders.

Seven cities in six different countries are participating, including Southend-on-Sea and Glasgow (UK), Uppsala (Sweden), Eindhoven (the Netherlands), Gdansk (Poland), Taipei (Taiwan) and Miami (USA).

During this phase, the project is assisting selected front-runner cities in identifying opportunities for initiating the Nexus approach, to develop and implement concrete project ideas (so-called 'urban living labs') and to establish a close dialogue between national and local governments.

The main focus is in developing a guiding conceptual framework to facilitate more cities to participate and to link the Urban Nexus to the United Nation's global 'New Urban Agenda' and SDGs (UN 2016). It has been recognised as essential to the future growth of the Urban Nexus to overcome the policy barriers that exist in some countries. Therefore, it mainly aims to assist cities and relevant stakeholders

Pathway for the Enabling Factors and Guiding Framework

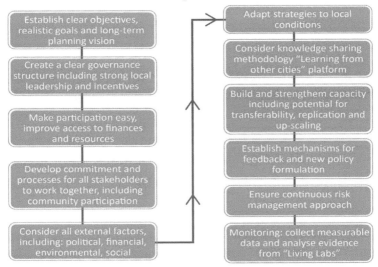

Fig. 4.3 Flow chart of the enabling factors for activating the EWFW Nexus, as identified by the author (2014a)

in mainstreaming and replicating the Nexus approach as a national initiative, implementing the principles of the circular economy.

How Does the Nexus Overlap with the Circular Economy?

The *Circular Economy* is defined as 'an economy which balances economic development with environmental and resources protection. It puts emphasis on the most efficient use and recycling/recovery of resources, and environmental protection. A circular economy features low consumption of energy, low emission of pollutants and high efficiency; it involves applying cleaner production processes and integrated resource-based planning for development in urban areas, industry and agriculture' (UN EP 2013: 16–18).

In contrast to an unsustainable linear economy, a Circular Economy is restorative and regenerative by design and can be seen as a practical solution to the emerging resource crunch which has resulted in growing tensions regarding geopolitics and supply risks, contributing to volatile and insecure conditions. The circular economy can help to stabilise these issues by decoupling economic and urban growth from resource consumption. Key principles of the circular economy are: to preserve and enhance natural capital by controlling finite stocks and balancing renewable resource flows, to optimise resource yields by designing for remanufacturing, refurbishing and recycling; to keep materials and components circulating and contributing to the economy; and to foster system effectiveness by revealing and designing out negative externalities (EMF 2017).

There are clear overlaps in both concepts, the Urban Nexus and the concept of a Circular Economy. The *decoupling* concept is key to the circular economy and urban metabolism concepts (as outlined in the *Hannover Principles* by McDonough and Braungart 1992, which led to the *Cradle-to-Cradle* concept, see Part I).

An attempt to decouple growth from the use of resources was successfully initiated in Curitiba (Brazil) in the 1990–2000s: Community-level decoupling was achieved through the exchange of recyclable waste for bus vouchers and fresh local produce, such as locally grown vegetables. Curitiba's Bus Rapid Transit (BRT) is a lower cost alternative to rail transit and is a part of Curitiba's 'closing the loop strategy'. 90 percent of Curitiba's residents are involved in daily recycling of their waste and achieve around a 70 percent recycling rate. This highly successful initiative creates a strong link between integrated public transport, waste recycling and job creation (including the empowerment of unemployed people).

I should note that the three key concepts (resource nexus, circular economy and decoupling) are not exactly the same—each has a slightly different focus—however, they all have resource efficiency of urban systems at their core. The multi-scale Nexus approach aims to contribute substantially to the resilience of cities. The importance of such an integrated approach has frequently been acknowledged and there is now increasing recognition of the dynamic interplay of resources and their supply systems in the urban context, such as the close interconnection that energy, water, food and material flows could provide as an opportunity for a 'policy nexus' to better integrate planning and resource management within and across urban boundaries, sectors and jurisdictions that can be translated into tangible, handbook-like insights for cities and regions elsewhere (Daher and Mohtar 2015).

The Need for Integration: The Resource Challenge of Our Urban Systems

The embodied energy and water contained in non-recovered materials pose a significant issue. For instance, biomass generation provides renewable energy, while nutrient cycling and urban farming in cities improves food security, rainfall catchment allows for aquifers to recharge, and the re-manufacturing of waste material recovers the embodied energy and helps to avoid further depletion of scarce or virgin materials. The addition of material flows in the Nexus assessment is supported by the seminal UN EP report (2013, Chapter 4): 'Urban material flows in cities in the developed and developing world'. How does the Nexus approach contribute to a resource-efficient city? (Table 4.1)

The effectiveness of the use of water and energy resources and the successful recovery of materials/waste is still limited and widely determined by the fragmentation of systems, availability of technology and by the type of resource management. If systems are integrated they provide benefits to each other. However, urban planning and transformation has not so far paid adequate attention to the resilience of city systems and appears poorly prepared to face adaptation and mitigation challenges through urban regeneration projects (Davoudi and Porter 2012; Davoudi 2014).

A good example is waste management. There are new waste management solutions that offer good opportunities for district-scale solutions for both solid waste and water, such as the underground vacuum system for solid waste collection as found in the district Hammarby Sjoestad (Stockholm). Beside vacuum systems, new developments could also consider industrial robots to move solid waste to a central collection point through utility channels. By putting waste into standardised containers that robots can move, neighbourhoods can adhere to the three-bin approach (organics, recyclables and landfill) while accommodating any change in the sorting regime. An anaerobic digester could turn the neighbourhood's organic waste into energy, while an onsite material recovery facility would process the remainder.

The proposed Nexus recognises these linkages and aims to better respond to the need for integrated policies and implementation mechanisms with systems optimisation through an approach to counter silo-thinking between the urban sectors, transforming the inefficient system and moving away from out-dated single-purpose solutions.

Table 4.1 The elements of the Urban Nexus (by the author 2018; after: Bizikova et al. 2013)

Energy security	– Stable and reliable energy supply relative to demand – Availability of energy supply from renewables – Supply sufficient to satisfy demand at given price
Water security	– Access to clean water – Water safety – Water affordability
Food security	– Production, distribution and availability of food – Affordable access to healthy food – Utilisation of food: nutritional value, social value and food safety – Food stability over time
Material flows and waste recovery	– Resource recovery of waste materials – Affordable recycling, reuse, repair and recovery – Avoidance of material waste and the minimisation of waste – Doing more with fewer materials, because materials are finite

A Brief Literature Review of Nexus Thinking

Looking at the current literature, it becomes obvious how much over the last decade, the food-water-energy nexus concept has emerged as an increasingly prominent global policy, governance and research field. Numerous articles were published to shed some light on the interdependencies of the domains.

For instance, it is frequently argued that out-dated urban governance and management practices, in which resources are managed in isolation by their respective sectoral departments, have resulted in wasteful fragmentation and a disconnect between infrastructure and governance mechanisms at the city and metropolitan level. In this context, the Nexus concept suggests moving from mono-sectoral planning and a fragmented infrastructure system towards more integrated resource cycles (Siddiqi and Anadon 2011; Hussey and Pittock 2012; Granit et al. 2012; Howells et al. 2013; Brandi et al. 2014; Gu et al. 2014; Mohtar 2016).

To sustainably govern the rural-urban linkages and resource interdependencies, it is increasingly recognized that an integrated approach to urban development and resource management is essential, both across sectors and across scales (Lehmann 2010a; Bennett et al. 2016). Strategies such as optimising supply chains and establishing cascades and cycles of resources between systems have been successfully tested by some few cities and are now ready for wider implementation (European Union Commission 2014).

Over the last ten years, the importance of the energy–water nexus has been recognised by a number of international institutions—such as the United Nations, the World Business Council for Sustainable Development, the World Economic Forum (to name a few), and individual national governments and multinational corporations—and has been featured prominently in discussions about the concept of a green, circular economy and a resource-efficient, regenerated city (Decker et al. 2010; Hoff 2011).

Bizikova et al. (2013) have developed a practical planning and decision-support framework for landscape investment and risk management in urban regeneration. The work confirmed that water, energy and food securities are interdependent and not easily disentangled. The researchers also found that any strategy that 'focuses on one part of the nexus without considering its interconnections risks serious unintended consequences' (2013: 1). They found that recent reviews (similar to Allan and Matthews 2016; Keulertz et al. 2016) emphasise that the critical asset sought in the land acquisition process is usually water because it is instrumental to higher land productivity and a prerequisite for urbanisation and agriculture.

Several authors argue that the nexus approach should not be limited to the three-way water-food-energy security concept but could also include other concerns such as land use, material flows and climate change (Scott et al. 2011; Rodriguez et al. 2013; UN ESCAP 2013; Sutherland et al. 2014; Vogt et al. 2014; Walker et al. 2014; Weitz et al. 2014; Villamayor-Tomas et al. 2015). Berkes et al. (2003) have extensively researched urban resilience and its complex relationship to social-ecological systems by drawing on expertise in ecology, ecological economics and political and social science to understand how human communities respond and adapt to change in their natural resources and systems. They found that such research requires bridging disciplines, political boundaries, and temporal and spatial scales. Karnib (2017) developed a quantitative assessment framework of the water-energy-food nexus that allows integrated assessment by considering all the WEF inter-sectoral linkages and competing demands for resources to evaluate future development scenarios.

The Nexus has had many different names, more recently with *Food Security* being mentioned first. In 2008, the World Economic Forum (WEF) commenced exploring nexus concepts and published a series of relevant papers on the topic (Allan 2003; Waughray 2011). The WEF considered the water-food-trade sub-nexus and the energy-climate change sub-nexus as essential for integrating into a grand nexus scheme; however, at this time the work failed to provide an accessible framework that identified the key issues and stakeholders in the important private-sector supply chains and waste management practice (Andrade et al. 2011; Allan and Matthews 2016; Lehmann 2018a).

Bulkeley and Betsill found that the implementation of sustainable and resource-efficient cities is mainly shaped by forms of policy and governance which stretch across geographical scales and beyond the boundary of the urban (2005). As a consequence, Allouche et al. (2014) asked if the nexus debate masks a bigger debate on resource inequality and access. They promote a mix of large-scale and small-scale systems and note: 'Responding to the emerging WEF nexus discourse, we seek to introduce a more dynamic perspective to water, energy and food security, and argue that a shift in governance is required towards also incorporating solutions where the limits to control are acknowledged' (2014: 1). They also argue that while it is difficult to disagree with a vision of integration between the systems there was some consensus about what exactly it might mean in reality. While some consider the nexus approach and framing to be too restrictive (eg. excluding climate change), other actors see it as linked to green economy or emphasise the value chain management. Albrechts (2010) pointed out the changing role of planners and that it is only by working backwards (reverse thinking, also called 'back-casting') that urban planning is able to open up new perspectives and take other directions.

Hernandez (2017) points out that a new web-based Nexus platform or tool 'will be useful to understand how the water-energy-food systems benefit from and impact on ecosystem services over their entire life cycles at multiple spatial scales'. Such a tool does not yet currently exist, however, CRUNCH aspires to develop one.

A number of published nexus frameworks, including those by Hoff (2011), Rasul (2014), the World Economic Forum (2008) and the Stockholm Environment Institute (2012), demonstrate varying definitions of the relationships between the energy-water-food-material flow elements and the range of potential responses within urban regeneration projects. Bizikova et al. (2013: 7) noted that the future challenges in water, energy and food security indicate that any nexus needs to be integrated and addressed in tandem to fully understand the nature of the relationships among the elements (the domains or sectors) and the consequences of their resulting impacts in other sectors or on health (WHO 2010).

Daher and Mohtar (2015) described in 'The Ultimate Nexus' how water, energy and food perform together as a main system that forms a nexus, and how the system transformation from silos to Nexus is best approached to achieve better resource management; they launched an online web tool at www.wefnexustool.org that allows the user to create and test different scenarios with varying self-sufficiencies. The tool's output includes a summary of parameters affecting the Nexus, including:

- Water requirements (in m^3)
- Local energy requirements (in kJ)
- Local carbon emissions (in tons of CO_2)
- Land requirements (in ha)
- Financial requirements (in QAR)
- Energy consumption through import/transport (in kJ)
- Carbon emissions through import (in tons of CO_2)

Stringer et al. (2014) combined the nexus approach with resilience thinking and launched a novel multi-scale framework with the aim to enable a more equitable and just access to resources and resilience outcomes. They hope that applying the framework across different social-ecological systems will enhance the understanding of factors that shape more equitable and just outcomes.

Biggs and colleagues (Biggs et al. 2015) have found that the water-energy-food nexus is being promoted as a conceptual tool for achieving sustainable urban development; however, they criticise that so far, these frameworks for implementing nexus thinking have failed to explicitly or adequately incorporate sustainable livelihoods perspectives. They mention that some of the results from researching the Nexus can already be seen, for example, in new technologies that are dramatically reducing the amount of food waste by composting and returning the nutrients to the soil, helping to make better use of both of those resources.

Key Lessons Learnt from the Cases

The main points learnt so far include:

- Beyond helping to improve resource-efficiency, it is essential to put a clear and reliable governance structure in place that ensures the longevity of the initiatives. This is supported by co-development with local stakeholders and the engagement of community groups to allow for participation and empowerment with agreed feedback mechanisms before the start of the regeneration project.

- The specific actions optimised different technological solutions that were integrated in the planning procedures using the multi-disciplinary Nexus approach.
- To be successful and ensure impact, all urban living labs (ULLs) could use a local and decentralised systems approach.

Relevance of the Nexus to the Transition of Urban Systems

In future, it is envisaged that new infrastructure for larger urban populations will allow for more decentralised systems that further improve the resource-efficiency of cities while dramatically reducing their resource consumption. Moving away from conventional centralised systems to a decentralised scale of operation (eg. where buildings generate their own energy), the Nexus will serve as a viable guideline for the better integration of decentralised energy and water infrastructure into urban form. Decentralised energy and water systems have increasingly been integrated into buildings and districts, and solar PV modules (in combination with large battery storage systems) have been enabling renewable energy to be used locally, contributing to the decarbonisation of cities and turning clusters of buildings into 'power-stations' that generate at least half of their own energy demand at the point of consumption (Lehmann 2014b). The combination of building-integrated photo-voltaic (PV) panels with battery storage systems allows buildings to produce and store their own energy or export their surplus energy, so that the buildings become independent from the energy grid (which is particularly helpful during peak energy demand periods).

Much of the infrastructure is ageing; for instance, it is estimated that 25 percent of water is wasted in U.S. cities due to leakages in the old water supply system.

Centralised water treatment facilities, power-stations and waste landfills are still reminiscent of the systems introduced during the industrial era, but are now being slowly replaced by new infrastructure for district-scale technologies with decentralised energy, water and waste management solutions. These new district scale technologies are often owned and operated by the utility companies, community cooperatives, housing associations or local governments. It allows districts to reduce their carbon emissions, their energy load (demand) on the electricity grid, and even become 'surplus districts' that can generate more energy than needed and feed energy back into the grid. Decentralised systems facilitate the integration of district-wide technologies including micro wind turbines, biomass and geothermal power (Lehmann 2010b; IRENA 2015). The following table shows some of the positive results that can be achieved through Nexus thinking (Table 4.2).

The Conceptual Problem with 'Decoupling Growth'; the Nexus' Key Messages So Far

The urban Nexus approach has now been widely introduced as one of the future methods for implementation of the UN's 'New Urban Agenda 2030' (UN 2016; Hák et al. 2016), which was developed with an emphasis on such synergies and innovative approaches. It is expected that the conceptual framework of the Urban Nexus will deliver a number of expected benefits (as listed in the previous Table) (Fig. 4.4).

It is widely acknowledged that health and well-being are directly connected with a well-planned and healthy built environment. But much of the economically-driven decision making has not supported the built environment to promote this (eg. think of overdeveloped neighbourhoods such as in Hong Kong). Knowing that the commonly used GDP-driven approach has frequently been at the expense of the ecosystem, better metrics are needed to account for the environmental impact of business decisions. It is now recognised as an impediment to sustainable development that most economic policies around the world are still driven by the goal of maximising economic growth through a singular, simplistic increase in GDP. The increase in economic growth will always mean an increase in the use of resources, which is not infinitely possible (Meadows et al. 1972). While most conventional economists endorse the idea that economic growth can be 'decoupled' from environmental impacts, and that the economy can keep growing without using more resources and exacerbating environmental problems (UN EP 2013)—decoupling may just be a delusion and not a viable solution (Ward et al. 2017).

Overall, the Urban Nexus is still a young, emerging concept that requires more clarification and testing, even for developed UK and European cities (Allouche et al. 2014).

Table 4.2 The results from the implementation of the Nexus research project, indicating the trade-offs between improved health and environmental benefits (by the author 2018)

Impacts	Expected results from Nexus integration
Regenerated neighbourhoods and derelict areas	Deprived and derelict neighbourhoods receive a boost from implementation of the Nexus and are regenerated socially and environmentally; active citizenship is empowered and strengthened, the social fabric is enhanced. Empowerment of residents; reduced crime and vandalism due to improved attractiveness of the area.
Improved health and well-being	Health risks, especially to the elderly and children due to urban heat, are reduced, and a comfortable ambient temperature is reinstated. Energy-efficient cooling through plants.
Enhanced inclusiveness of public space, reducing social conflict	Improved access to high-quality green spaces (ranging from parks to small pocket or community gardens to green roofs) leads to more integrated planning processes for an ageing population and happier urban residents. Uneven access to public green spaces is avoided. Cultural benefits, including the city's attractiveness and overall satisfaction; as a result, the percentage of citizens involved in greening projects and park maintenance has increased.
Ecological benefits, including reduced risk of urban heat and flooding	Improved climate adaptation (temperature decrease in summer) of urban areas to climate-risks such as urban heat islands or urban flooding is mitigated; the delivery of eco-system services is enhanced and restored. Increased energy demand for cooling is avoided. Flood retention measures include ponds, constructed wetlands and green roofs for an increase in local water retention.
Strengthened urban resilience	Increased resource efficiency: the principles of a circular economy can be adopted towards a more resource-efficient city. Even increase in property values is possible.
Guidance from high-quality research outputs	Scientific peer-reviewed papers, publications and presentations. Open-access databases containing analytics of empirical data.

(continued)

Table 4.2 (continued)

Impacts	Expected results from Nexus integration
Policy development impact for governmental officials and practitioners	Capacity building. Policy briefs for participating cities and various digital tailored outcomes available online. Validation of the novel assessment framework of inclusive neighbourhood regeneration and identification of the challenges of the Nexus integration and operation. For the end-user target groups in the cities engaged in the pilot neighbourhoods, they will also be a part of co-creating strategies for inclusive neighbourhood regeneration.

Fig. 4.4 Developing a conceptual framework for the Food-Water-Energy-Waste Nexus with the effecting parameters, defining the major flows within and between natural and built systems, in regard to the natural supply and human demand (by the author 2018)

The Expected Results from Implementing the Urban Nexus

Here two practical examples for activating the nexus that cities could do:

- The city collects its organic waste and food waste (biomass) for two processes: firstly, for anaerobic digestion to generate renewable energy; secondly, for composting to return nutrients to the soil.
- The city produces renewable energy (solar) at a public space and collects rainwater for two processes: the energy is used to load batteries of a e-bike rental scheme located at this public space; secondly, the rainwater is collected through a sustainable drainage system and bio-filtration swales and stored to use for irrigation of urban greenery.

These are not theoretical ideas of a faraway future. Both examples are at the heart of what the Food-Water-Energy Nexus is about, and can be implemented by cities today, as the technology is available and economic payback from the investment is likely after a few years (Lehmann 2018b).

The development of a sustainable, resource efficient and competitive economy will increasingly require an accelerated transition to a more circular economic model, with products, processes and business models that are designed to maximise the value and utility of resources while at the same time reducing adverse health and environmental impacts. However, cities are likely to continue to struggle in their transition to implement a full circular economy model, properly stimulate regenerative practices and alter established urban consumption patterns.

Future urban regeneration projects will need innovative solutions for closing the loop across the nexus, while reducing material and resource flows and stimulating sound management of trade-offs and synergies among sectors. The focus would need to become more 'circular' by achieving:

- An increased recycling rate for end-of-life materials, to reduce landfill and incineration.
- Development of buildings and products designed for durability, repair and reuse, with markets based on durability.
- Improved environmental performance of the operations and a better recovery of resources from waste.

- Significantly reduced use of water from freshwater sources, and improved recovery of wastewater resources.
- Reduced natural resource consumption in urban and peri-urban areas and environmental footprint of cities as well as enhanced regenerative and productive capacity by integrating green spaces;
- Increased repair maintenance, reuse (including sharing), remanufacturing and recycling of products, buildings and materials, which will enhance urban resilience.

References

Alberti, M. (2005). The Effects of Urban Patterns on Ecosystem Function. *International Regional Science Review, 28*(2), 168–192.

Albrechts, L. (2010). More of the Same Is Not Enough! How Could Strategic Spatial Planning Be Instrumental in Dealing with the Challenges Ahead? *Environment and Planning B: Planning and Design, 37*(6), 1115–1127.

Allan, J. A. (2003). Virtual Water – the Water, Food, and Trade Nexus: Useful Concept or Misleading Metaphor?, International Water Resources Association. *Water International, 28*(1), 4–11.

Allan, J. A., & Matthews, N. (2016). The Water-Energy-Food Nexus and Ecosystems: The Political Economy. In F. Dodds & J. Bertram (Eds.), *The Water, Food, Energy and Climate Nexus: Challenges and an Agenda for Action*. London: Routledge.

Allouche, J., Middleton, C., & Gyawal, D. (2014). *Nexus Nirvana or Nexus Nullity? A Dynamic Approach to Security and Sustainability in the Water-Energy-Food Nexus*. Working Paper. Online. Retrieved March 10, 2017, from www.steps-centre.org

Andrade, Á., Córdoba, R., Dave, R., Girot, P., Herrera-F, B., Munroe, R., Oglethorpe, J., Pramova, E., Watson, J., & Vergara, W. (2011). Draft Principles and Guidelines for Integrating Ecosystem-Based Approaches to Adaptation in Project and Policy Design: A Discussion Document. In *IUCNCEM, CATIE, 30pp* (p. 27). Costa Rica: Turrialba.

Arezki, R., Deininger, K., & Selod, H. (2015). What Drives the Global "Land Rush"? *The World Bank Economic Review, 29*(2), 207–233.

Bazilian, M., Rogner, H., Howells, M., Hermann, S., Arent, D., Gielen, D., & Yumkella, K. K. (2011). Considering the Energy, Water and Food Nexus: Towards an Integrated Modelling Approach. *Energy Policy, 39*(12), 7896–7906.

Bennett, G., Cassin, J., & Carroll, N. (2016). Natural Infrastructure Investment and Implications for the Nexus: A Global Overview. *Ecosystem Services, 17*, 293–297.

Berkes, F., Colding, J., et al. (2003). *Navigating Social-Ecological Systems: Building Resilience for Complexity*. Cambridge: Cambridge University.

Biggs, E. M., Bruce, E., Boruff, B., Duncan, J. M., Horsley, J., Pauli, N., & Haworth, B. (2015). Sustainable Development and the Water–Energy–Food Nexus: A Perspective on Livelihoods. *Environmental Science & Policy, 54*, 389–397.

Bizikova, L., Roy, D., Swanson, D., Venema, H. D., & McCandless, M. (2013). *The Water-Energy-Food Security Nexus: Towards a Practical Planning and Decision-Support Framework for Landscape Investment and Risk Management.* International Institute for Sustainable Development.

Brandi, C. A., Richerzhagen, C., & Stepping, K. M. (2014). *Post 2015: Why Is the Water-Energy-Land Nexus Important for the Future Development Agenda?* United Nations Post-2015 Agenda for Global Development: Perspectives from China and Europe, German Development Institute/Deutsches Institut für Entwicklungspolitik (DIE), Bonn, pp. 297–310.

Bringezu, S., & Bleischwitz, R. (2009). *Sustainable Resource Management: Global Trends, Visions and Policies.* Greenleaf Publishing.

Bulkeley, H., & Betsill, M. (2005). Rethinking Sustainable Cities: Multilevel Governance and the 'Urban' Politics of Climate Change. *Environmental Politics, 14*(1).

Daher, B. T., & Mohtar, R. H. (2015). Water–Energy–Food (WEF) Nexus Tool 2.0: Guiding Integrative Resource Planning and Decision-Making. *Water International, 40*(5–6), 748–771.

Davoudi, S. (2014). Climate Change, Securitisation of Nature, and Resilient Urbanism. *Environment and Planning C – Government and Policy 2014, 32*(2), 360–375.

Davoudi, S., & Porter, L. (2012). Urban Resilience: What Does It Mean in Planning Practice? *Planning Theory & Practice, 13*(2). https://doi.org/10.1080/14649357.2012.67 7124.

Decker, E. H., Elliott, S., Smith, F. A., Blake, D. R., & Rowland, F. S. (2010). Energy and Material Flow Through the Urban Ecosystem. *Annual Review of Energy and the Environment, 25*, 685–740.

Ellen MacArthur Foundation, EMF. (2014/2017). *The Circular Economy. A Wealth of Flows* (2nd ed.). Ellen MacArthur Foundation Publishing. Online. Retrieved July 10, 2018, from https://www.ellenmacarthurfoundation.org/publications/the-circular-economy-a-wealth-of-flows-2nd-edition

European Union Commission. (2014). *Horizon 2020 Societal Challenge 5: 'Climate Action, Environment, Resource Efficiency and Raw Materials' Advisory Group Report.*

Foley, J., et al. (2011). Solutions for a Cultivated Planet. *Nature, 478*, 337–342.

Folke, C. (2006). Resilience: Emergence of a Perspective for Social–Ecological Systems. *Global Environmental Change, 16*(3), 253–267.

Gold, H. D., & Bass, J. (2010). Energy-Water Nexus: Socioeconomic Considerations and Suggested Legal Reforms in the Southwest. *Natural Resources Journal, 50*, 563.

Granit, J., Jägerskog, A., Lindström, A., Björklund, G., Bullock, A., Löfgren, R., & Pettigrew, S. (2012). Regional Options for Addressing the Water, Energy and Food Nexus in Central Asia and the Aral Sea Basin. *International Journal of Water Resources Development, 28*(3), 419–432.

Gu, A., Teng, F., & Wang, Y. (2014). China Energy-Water Nexus: Assessing the Water-Saving Synergy Effects of Energy-Saving Policies During the Eleventh Five-Year Plan. *Energy Conversion and Management, 85*, 630–637.

Hák, T., Janoušková, S., & Moldan, B. (2016). Sustainable Development Goals: A Need for Relevant Indicators. *Ecological Indicators, 60*, 565–573.

Hernandez, E. M. (2017). *The Role of Ecosystem Services in the Water-Energy-Food Nexus*. NERC Project (UK). Online. Retrieved March 10, 2017, from http://nercgw4plus. ac.uk/project/role-of-ecosystem-services-in-the-water-energy-food-nexus/

Hoff, H. (2011). *Understanding the Nexus*. Background Paper for the Bonn, Germany, 2011 Nexus Conference.

Howells, M., Hermann, S., Welsch, M., Bazilian, M., Segerström, R., Alfstad, R., Gielen, D., Rogner, H., Fischer, G., van Velthuizen, H., Wiberg, D., Young, C., Roehrl, A., Mueller, A., Steduto, P., & Ramma, I. (2013). Integrated Analysis of Climate Change, Land-Use, Energy and Water Strategies. *Nature Climate Change, 3*, 621–626.

Hussey, K., & Pittock, J. (2012). The Energy–Water Nexus: Managing the Links between Energy and Water for a Sustainable Future. *Ecology and Society, 17*(1), 31.

Intergovernmental Panel on Climate Change (IPCC). (2015). *Fifth Assessment Report, Chapter 13*, Geneva.

IRENA. (2015). *Renewable Energy in the Water, Energy and Food Nexus*. Abu Dhabi, United Arab Emirates: The International Renewable Energy Agency.

Karnib, A. (2017). A Quantitative Assessment Framework for Water, Energy and Food Nexus. *Computational Water, Energy, and Environmental Engineering, 6*, 11–23.

Keulertz, M., Sowers, J., Woertz, E., & Mohtar, R. (2016). The Water–Food–Energy *Nexus*: An Introduction to *Nexus* Concepts and some Conceptual and Operational Problems; WEF Nexus Research Group. In *The Oxford Handbook of Water Politics and Policy*. Oxford, UK: Oxford University Press.

Lehmann, S. (2010a). *The Principles of Green Urbanism. Transforming the City for Sustainability*. London: Earthscan Publishing.

Lehmann, S. (2010b). Green Urbanism: Formulating a Series of Holistic Principles. *S.A.P.I.E.N.S – Surveys and Perspectives Integrating Environment and Society, 3*(2), 53–72.

Lehmann, S. (2014a). Green Districts and Carbon Engineering: Increasing Greenery, Reducing Heat Island Effects. In S. Lehmann (Ed.), *Low Carbon Cities. Transforming Urban Systems* (pp. 191–209). London: Routledge.

Lehmann, S. (2014b). Low Carbon Districts: Mitigating the Urban Heat Island with Green Roof Infrastructure. *City, Culture & Society, 5*(1), 1–8. https://doi.org/10.1016/j. ccs.2014.02.002.

Lehmann, S. (2018a). Implementing the Urban Nexus Approach for Improved Resource-Efficiency of Developing Cities in Southeast-Asia. *City, Culture and Society, 13*(6), 46–56.

Lehmann, S. (2018b). Conceptualizing the Urban Nexus Framework for a Circular Economy: Linking Energy, Water, Food and Waste in Southeast-Asian Cities. In P. Droege (Ed.), *Renewable Strategies for Cities and Regions. Urban Energy Transition 2* (pp. 371–398). Amsterdam, Netherlands: Elsevier.

McDonough, W., & Braungart, M. (1992). *The Hannover Principles: Design for Sustainability*. Commissioned Report for the Hannover EXPO, Germany. Online.

Meadows, D. H., Meadows, D. L., Randers, J., & Behrens, W. (1972). *The Limits to Growth: A Report to the Club of Rome's Project on the Predicament of Mankind*. New York, NY: Universe Books (1971 Report/1972 Book).

Mohtar, R. H. (2016). *The Water-Energy-Food Nexus: Who Owns It?* Online Policy Brief-16/11 (April 2016), OCP Policy Center, Rabat, Morocco.

Potschin, M., Kretsch, C., Haines-Young, R., Furman, E., Berry, P., & Baró, F. (2016). Nature-based Solutions. In M. Potschin & K. Jax (Eds.), *OpenNESS Ecosystem Services Reference Book*. European Centre for Nature Conservation.

Rasul, G. (2014). Food, Water, and Energy Security in South Asia: A Nexus Perspective from the Hindu Kush Himalayan Region. *Environmental Science & Policy, 39*, 35–48.

Rodriguez, D. J., Delgado, A., DeLaquil, P., & Sohns, A. (2013). *Thirsty Energy*. Water Paper. Washington, DC: World Bank.

Schneider, A., Friedl, M. A., & Potere, D. (2009). A New Map of Global Urban Extent from MODIS Satellite Data. *Environmental Research Letters, 4*, 044003.

Scott, C. A., Pierce, S. A., Pasqualetti, M. J., Jones, A. L., Montz, B. E., & Hoover, J. H. (2011). Policy and Institutional Dimensions of the Water–Energy Nexus. *Energy Policy, 39*(10), 6622–6630.

Siddiqi, A., & Anadon, L. D. (2011). The Water–Energy Nexus in Middle East and North Africa. *Energy Policy, 39*(8), 4529–4540.

Stockholm Environment Institute. (2012). Reducing Greenhouse Gas Emissions Associated with Consumption: A Methodology for Scenario Analysis. Report Available Online. Retrieved from https://www.jstor.org/stable/resrep00529

Stringer, L. C., et al. (2014). *Combining Nexus and Resilience Thinking in a Novel Framework to Enable More Equitable and just Outcomes*. Sustainability Research Institute Paper No 73, SRI-Papers Online, University of Leeds, UK.

Sutherland, W. J., Gardner, T., Bogich, T. L., Bradbury, R. B., Clothier, B., Jonsson, M., Kapos, V., Lane, S. N., Miller, I., Schroeder, M., Spalding, M., Spencer, T., White, P. C. L., & Dicks, L. V. (2014). Solution Scanning as a Key Policy Tool: Identifying Management Interventions to Help Maintain and Enhance Regulating Ecosystem Services. *Ecology and Society, 19*(2), 1–22.

UN EP. (2013). *City-Level Decoupling: Urban Resource Flows and the Governance of Infrastructure Transitions*. A Report of the Working Group on Cities of the International Resource Panel. Authors include: Swilling, M., Robinson, B., Marvin, S., & Hodson, M. Online. Retrieved March 10, 2017, from http://web.unep.org/ourplanet/october-2016/unep-publications/city-level-decoupling

UN ESCAP. (2011). *Statistical Yearbook for Asia and the Pacific 2011*. United Nations Economic and Social Commission for Asia and the Pacific, Bangkok, Thailand.

UN ESCAP. (2013). *United Nations Economic and Social Commission for Asia and the Pacific. The Status of the Water-Food-Energy Nexus in Asia and the Pacific*. Discussion Paper United Nations, Bangkok, Thailand.

United Nations (UN). (2016). *Sustainable Development Goals* and *New Urban Agenda: Key Commitments*. Online. Retrieved March 10, 2017, from http://www.un.org/sustainabledevelopment/ and http://www.un.org/sustainabledevelopment/blog/2016/10/newurbanagenda/

Villamayor-Tomas, S., Grundmann, P., Epstein, G., Evans, T., & Kimmich, C. (2015). The Water-Energy-Food Security Nexus Through the Lenses of the Value Chain and the Institutional Analysis and Development Frameworks. *Water Alternatives, 8*(1), 735–755.

Vogt, C., Schlenk, J. C., Horne, C., & Gügel, C. (2014). Operationalizing the Urban NEXUS Towards Resource-Efficient and Integrated Cities and Metropolitan Regions: Case Studies. *Deutsche Gesellschaft für Internationale Zusammenarbeit (GIZ) GmbH.*

Walker, R. V., Beck, M. B., Hall, J. W., Dawson, R. J., & Heidrich, O. (2014). The Energy-Water-Food Nexus: Strategic Analysis of Technologies for Transforming the Urban Metabolism. *Journal of Environmental Management, 141,* 104–115.

Ward, J., Chiveralls, K., Fioramonti, L., Sutton, P., & Costanza, R. (2017). The Decoupling Delusion: Rethinking Growth and Sustainability. *The Conversation,* 12 March 2017. Online. Retrieved March 20, 2018, from https://theconversation.com/the-decoupling-delusion-rethinking-growth-and-sustainability-71996

Waughray, D. (2011). *Water Security: The Water–Food–Energy–Climate Nexus.* The World Economic Forum Water Initiative. Island Press, USA. Retrieved from www.wefnexustool.org

Weitz, N., Nilsson, M., & Davis, M. (2014). A Nexus Approach to the Post-2015 Agenda: Formulating Integrated Water, Energy, and Food SDGs. *SAIS Review of International Affairs, 34,* 37–50.

Wold Economic Forum. (2008/2011). *The Water-Food-Energy-Climate Nexus.* Report available online. Retrieved March 20, 2018, from http://www3.weforum.org/docs/WEF_WI_WaterSecurity_WaterFoodEnergyClimateNexus_2011.pdf and www.wefnexustool.org

World Health Organization (WHO). (2010). *UN-Water Global Assessment of Sanitation and Drinking Water: Targeting Resources for Better Results.* Geneva: World Health Organization.

Related Web Resources

The CRUNCH Project. Retrieved from. www.fwe-nexus.eu

The Nexus Network, ESRC-Supported Web Site. (2015). UK. Retrieved from www.thenexusnetwork.org

World Economic Forum. Retrieved from. www.wefnexustool.org

5

The Ten Strategies for an Urban Regeneration

Why an Urban Manifesto for UK Cities?

Successful urban regeneration will be the result of a collective vision, realised through creative and enduring relationships between the community, government, developers, academia and professionals involved in its design, delivery, governance and maintenance. Strategic thinking about our cities, what they should look like and how they should perform, is more important than ever.

With an appreciation of the range of stakeholders with interests in urban renewal, and their contrasting roles and perspectives, there is a wide range of urban regeneration typologies. The *Urban Manifesto* will help to make informed decisions around built form and the benefits of a more strategic approach. Here are the much-needed ten strategies for urban regeneration, the core message of this book.

The following strategies for urban regeneration are recommended:

Strategy 1.
Urban culture and heritage: maintaining local character and a unique sense of place
Strategy 2.
A public space network for a compact, walkable and mixed-use city
Strategy 3.
Energy-efficient, clean and convenient mobility

© The Author(s) 2019
S. Lehmann, *Urban Regeneration*, https://doi.org/10.1007/978-3-030-04711-5_5

Strategy 4.
Coastal cities: transforming the waterfront of resilient, future-proof cities
Strategy 5.
Inclusive mixed-used urban living
Strategy 6.
High-quality architectural design and public space as a catalyst for a better city
Strategy 7.
Smart citizens, smart energy and citizen participation
Strategy 8.
Thinking long-term and making the most of what we have
Strategy 9.
Developing vibrant university quarters to regenerate the heart of our cities
Strategy 10.
Cities sharing their experiences, learning from each other: new knowledge
    platforms

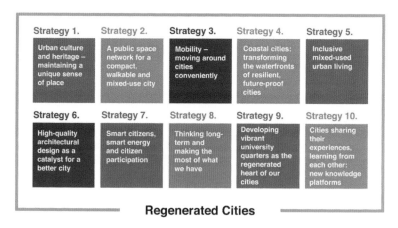

Fig. 5.1 Diagram of the 10 Strategies that need to be tackled simultaneously

The City is the very mirror of life. You only have to cast your eyes on buildings to feel the presence of the past, the spirit of a place; they are the reflection of society.—**I. M. Pei**

Strategy 1.

Urban Culture and Heritage: Maintaining Local Character and a Unique Sense of Place

Maintaining the fine grain of a city and its urban fabric creates a continuous transformation linking to the city's past and sense of place as a shared and refined urban vision. The cultures of the people and ecology of the place must be expressed at a human scale through both physical and social structures.

Coherence, not spectacle:

Looking to the past for context is vital to the design of successful public spaces. The distinctive cultural identity, diversity and full potential of the community should be supported spiritually, physically and visually to sustain a sense of collective ownership, belonging and civic pride.

The design of spaces and buildings is always influenced by their context, enhancing local character and heritage and regional food. Simultaneously responding to current-day needs, changes in society and cultural diversity, contemporary places can have a deep sense of the city's history and heritage.

In this context, architecture can be transformative in its localities without sparking gentrification.

Responding to demographic change, the significance of 'place' and social diversity needs more attention.

Resisting the homogenising impact of globalisation will make our cities better places to live.

Increasing biodiversity within the city also is important: natural areas and parks must be easily accessible and in close proximity to citizens.

Developing community and neighbourhood resilience is a pathway to resilience for the whole city.

Green spaces, community gardens and urban farming can play a huge role in delivering ecological and social functions within cities. Preserving green space and re-naturing strategies are important factors for any city (with benefits ranging from a reduction in greenhouse gas emissions and air pollution to a reduction in obesity).

A public realm that puts people first and is vibrant all year-round.

Strategy 2.

A Public Space Network for a Compact, Walkable and Mixed-Use City

Creating calm, walkable streetscapes and a network of inter-connected public spaces is the 'glue' needed to hold the different parts of the city centre together. Mixed-use places are more active a higher percentage of time and avoid commercial zones that go 'dead' after 6 pm in the evening.

Acknowledging the social dimensions of the traditional street, vibrant streets and urban spaces with their own distinct character can form a coherent interconnected network of places that support walking, social interaction and display distinctive private, commercial and civil functions.

Nature-sensitive urban strategies and a greener city will help to increase biodiversity, absorb CO_2 emissions and improve public health and well-being; this includes the use of sustainable drainage systems and permeable ground surfaces across the city.

We want to create policy and incentives to make urban forests, green roofs, improvement of open spaces, community gardens and food production a part of the city's future. Part of the strategy is to repurpose omitted roofs as contemporary public spaces.

We need to design permeable streets for pedestrians: the pedestrian environment should be closely associated with active frontages at street level, so there can be an appropriate intensity of use at all times. Essential activities must be accessible or within walking distance and there should be a concentration of activity around meeting places, including growing food locally.

The public realm must be age-friendly and supported by inclusive processes that respond to the local community and its changing economic and social conditions.

Bridging heavy industrial corridors, new types of infrastructure and public spaces can be delivered. The continuous upgrading of public space to provide opportunities ensuring connectivity and social inclusion are strong themes throughout the urban future.

*The presence of buildings around a park is important in design. They enclose it. They make a definite shape out of the space.—***Jane Jacobs**

Strategy 3.

Energy-Efficient, Clean and Convenient Mobility

We need to walk more and drive less for our own health and the health of the ecosystem, and better walking routes within the city are essential. Cycling highways will make it possible to cycle entirely separately from cars and trucks.

Healthy ageing in the city:

A permeable street network with pedestrian priority gives maximum freedom of movement, making walking and cycling enjoyable and safe while in turn making it the preferred mode of transport and offering a good choice of active transport.

Streets and public spaces are the 'glue' that holds society together. Mobility is the 'oil' that brings people together.

Strengthening connectivity and removing walls and fences will play an important part in enhancing the city's connectivity and resilience.

Lessen the need to commute, making transportation more equitable and identify new region-wide mobility concepts that are not car-based, such as enabling young adults to travel freely by public transport to open up opportunities for education and jobs.

Cities must have fewer cars on their roads to ease congestion, reduce air pollution and noise, by using alternative forms of transport including public transport, in the form of buses and light railway, on-demand minibus services, car-sharing schemes, e-bikes, cycling and walking.

We need a mobility system that is safer, low-carbon and more convenient than the private car, at much lower cost.

Electric mobility will significantly reduce air pollution and noise in the city. Could we ban combustion engine cars in our city centres by 2030?

Adding highway lanes to deal with traffic congestion is like loosening your belt to cure obesity.—**Lewis Mumford**

Strategy 4.

Coastal Cities: Transforming the Waterfront of Resilient, Future-Proof Cities

Although completely 'future-proofing' a city is impossible, we can strategically plan ahead and allow the city to become more adaptable and anticipate demands and impacts to ensure future infrastructure is resilient.

New and existing public places must respect, enhance and respond to the local natural environment within and around them.

Strengthening the city's readiness to deal with the impact of rising sea-levels: Alongside protection from the dangers of sea-level rise, urban parks and other landscaped areas along the waterfront should provide space for recreation, increased biodiversity and help support a balanced environment.

Revitalising coastal cities with reinvigorated waterfronts: ports, beaches, marinas and esplanades.

Enhancing the seafront with a board-walk, soft landscaping and dykes such as in the Netherlands, where sea-level rise challenges are resolved by clever landscaping design, is usually a better solution than hard-engineered seawalls.

Increasing community participation in the planning process: Decision-making for the ongoing development and management of the future waterfront and urban fabric must engage stakeholders and the local community through public participation.

A city is more than a place in space, it is a drama in time.—**Patrick Geddes**

Strategy 5.

Inclusive Mixed-Used Urban Living

We cannot allow cities to sprawl in an uncoordinated way or expand into greenfield sites. There are over 60,000 hectares of brownfield land in UK cities which already have strong transport links to trains and trams. We need to engage more in infill development of already built-up areas before encroaching on green belts or greenfield sites. Building more fringe suburbs would lead to increased car use and the risk of emptying out existing cities.

The city must provide a diversity of functions, tenure, facilities and services, with a mix of building designs and types. It should include a variety of appropriately scaled neighbourhoods catering to different socio-economic groups and encouraging a better use of roof spaces.

A diverse, accessible, affordable and active city will encourage successful commercial activity, promote prosperity and support the well-being of inhabitants including the ageing population.

Architects can help prevent gentrification through well-balanced residential and non-residential mixed-use developments that reduce travel and support inclusion, for instance by designing homes that people can progressively upgrade or expand over time, as they can afford it.

The built environment must also seek to minimise the use of carbon-intensive products, energy and non-renewable resources. There are new ways of building using off-site construction and design competitions.

Modular houses that are built off-site are a way to extend housing choices and open up innovative models for urban infill and careful densification.

Household sizes will continue to decrease.

Modular off-site manufactured housing can deliver homes faster and to a higher quality and reduce construction waste.

The supply of good housing is essential for growth, including a decent standard of multi-generational family housing.

Cities that manage density well will enrich the lives of people who live and work there. Urban form and good building design are also significant drivers of resource efficiency and neighbourhood regeneration.

What is the city but the people?—**William Shakespeare**

Strategy 6.

High-Quality Architectural Design and Public Space as a Catalyst for a Better City

Urban regeneration is also an aesthetic and social issue. Architecture has to be more than individual acts: it has to provide a coherent background. You cannot create a city from 'iconic' foreground buildings, otherwise you will get a circus of attention-seeking self-referential buildings (like in Dubai for instance).

Architecture is a continuously developing public language.

Design must be at the heart of any urban planning, creating a human-scale built environment, higher design standards and raising the overall quality of our architectural culture.

The best way to achieve the shift to carbon-neutral buildings and higher quality architectural design is through design contest—where a solution is sought from a well-defined and agreed brief.

We should use the development of publicly-owned land to pioneer the best sustainable designs and be effective champions of the importance of good architecture. Leading by example: city councils and universities can collaborate as transformation agents, supporting design culture (with design competitions for all projects of £0.5mill+ on municipal land).

Encouraging the reuse and up-cycling of existing buildings and structures and the careful increase in urban density will help to make the city more authentic and sustainable, which can include mixed-use neighbourhoods such as apartments on top of shopping malls, enabling people to live in or close to the city centre.

Infill through careful densification requires setting high design standards with a coherence in building heights and the use of materials and colour—with a plurality of aesthetic approaches being offered.

Sustainable cities are compact, intensive and diverse. The use of local materials can give a place its homogeneity and distinctive character.

Architecture is about public space held by buildings.—**Richard Rogers**

Strategy 7.

Smart Citizens, Smart Energy and Citizen Participation

Everyone has a right to the city. Strengthening public participation in decision making and creating inclusive public spaces is an important goal. Smart, citizen-centric planning will use urban performance data for better-informed decision-making and new policy formulation.

This includes an accelerated transition to clean, renewable energy generated in the city, and the integration of emerging technologies. Digital urbanism can be used to model and forecast the impacts of decisions on urban living.

To activate the water-energy-food nexus, new green infrastructure and nature-based solutions are required that include sustainable drainage systems, smart electricity grids and concepts based on the principles of a circular economy.

Instead of 'planning in silos', the inclusion of citizens and the importance of realising young people's values is essential for a regenerated urban future.

The smart city approach (tech-enabled, but not tech-centred): working more closely with universities will allow cities to make the most out of digitisation (ranging from intelligent traffic systems, to data harvesting, to car-sharing on demand, to drone mapping, to virtual reality for neighbourhood regeneration and scenario testing).

Data collection and analysis technology is a key enabler of solutions that will make cities more sustainable and responsive.

Measuring urban sustainability progress is essential to be sure we are on the right trajectory.

The word citizen has to do with cities, and the ideal city is organised around citizenship – around participation in public life.—**Rebecca Solnit**

Strategy 8.

Thinking Long-Term and Making the Most of What We Have

Optimising urban density and exploring alternative scenarios will enhance the city. An increase in low density development leads to too many car trips and inefficiencies. New thinking about compact, higher density living around transport hubs and above shopping centres is necessary.

The contradictory objectives need to be carefully balanced: How people want to live versus the imperatives of sustainability targets.

Gaining community trust and buy-in for higher density architecture is vital. We cannot increase density without community support.

Land value is critical. How can we better capture the increase in land value from public investment and planning permission?

Great street, great place, great neighbourhood: In urban regeneration long-term thinking is essential. Too much focus on the short run does not contribute to solving social disparities.

Undoubtedly, the greatest asset of cities are the existing buildings, the old and new, and the combination of history and density. The adaptive reuse of historical buildings in combination with contemporary extensions provides a good model, and a chance to prioritise construction on brownfield rather than greenfield sites.

Re-purposing of old buildings: Taking full advantage of the existing and making the most of what we have, while creating 'Spaces of Opportunity' is a sustainable way to strengthen the city and repair discontinuity.

Density and mixed-use creates
urbanity.—**Renzo Piano**

Strategy 9.

Developing Vibrant University Quarters to Regenerate the Heart of Our Cities

If the City is the most significant creation of humankind, the University is still one of the most important institutions created by society for the advancement of civilisation. Re-imagine a regenerated city centre that is less car dominated, with walkable public space and a world class university quarter at its centre.

University patronage is frequently behind the best architecture in the UK.

Fit for the future; creating a campus that has a long life, loose fit approach and strong pedestrian connectivity with public spaces that provide moments of calm in the city centre.

New urban forms should be capable of adaptation over time to meet changing needs and to promote the continued use of existing buildings and resources.

Campus greening initiatives could include energy efficient buildings, urban farming, bike sharing programmes and renewable energy generation. Key design elements include the creation of active public spaces at ground level that engage with the city and use of glazed elements to emphasize 24/7 activity on the campus.

The new university quarters will be integrated into their surrounding community, with transparent ground-floors that allow for greater permeability

and visibility of activities and the integration of public uses, with new informal spaces between buildings for interaction and learning.

Universities should develop 'Innovation Quarters' and reduce car-centric situations by increasing the provision of secure cycle racks and further promote bicycle usage and cycling by staff and students.

Great streets make great cities!—Jane Jacobs

Strategy 10.

Cities Sharing Their Experiences, Learning from Each Other: New Knowledge Platforms

The role of social innovation, collaboration and entrepreneurship in cities has to be recognised. There has to be space provided for alternative economies to thrive, supporting small-scale entrepreneurship which will benefit all.

Addressing the challenges of climate change through better urban development: Compact well-connected cities are more walkable, allowing for active zero-emission mobility such as walking, cycling and e-bikes.

Participatory and people-centred urban governance will lead to people-centred planning, and further improve the liveability and competitiveness of our cities by encouraging practices that make them more just, safe, healthy and resilient.

Concepts of co-creation, empowerment and community engagement play a significant role in the regeneration of our cities.

To change policy at the urban level and increase capacity, we can create a network of cities with new knowledge platforms that support better decision making, allowing cities to learn from each other and enhance impact.

We need more research with a strong focus on improving the environmental performance of neighbourhoods and communities by introducing the concept of 'integrated urban climate resilience'. The integration of technologies can further optimise the resource-efficient city, including end-user driven system integration (including different age and user groups).

By far the greatest and most admirable form of wisdom is that needed to plan and beautify cities and human communities.—**Socrates**

6

Examples of the Ten Urban Regeneration Strategies in Practice

Some Selected Examples Where the Strategies Have Been Applied

In this part, the Urban Manifesto lays out a set of urban regeneration design principles. To underpin the ten strategies, the book presents examples of thirteen UK cities that have tested these design principles. It illustrates positive cases where the strategies were adopted and put into reality.

The cases show that urban regeneration has the capacity to solve multiple problems simultaneously (eg. social equity and human health issues, carbon emission reductions and infrastructure, liveability and housing). While the post-war ambition was expressed in the New Towns of the 1960s, today we appreciate the careful densification and subtle stitching of building and place. The rich industrial heritage plays a major part in the resourceful regeneration of UK cities. It seems unbelievable that there are still plenty of areas in our towns and cities that are vacant or under-utilised without sufficient intensity of activity.

Frequently, urban regeneration strategies also underpin the concept of spatial restructuring, and the regeneration of port cities is always a special case (often with sea-level rise as key challenge), eg. how does the maritime heritage that makes these places so unique play a role in the projects? Local architects and planners embrace

© The Author(s) 2019
S. Lehmann, *Urban Regeneration*, https://doi.org/10.1007/978-3-030-04711-5_6

the site-specific vernacular with skill and care, using locally sourced materials such as clay tiles, bricks, locally grown timber and flint which provide a sense of scale, texture and locality.

The drivers and processes of urban spatial restructuring include market-driven processes and the potential roles and forms of government or municipal intervention in influencing such restructuring. New partners and stakeholders are getting involved, for instance, regional universities can be the drivers of renewal, regenerating towns and cities, and their role cannot be overestimated. Most campuses are embedded in the city and create civic spaces and insert significant new buildings into the existing fabric.

Architects are leading the involvement of citizens as they frequently possess an ability to bring people and processes together: They combine tradition with progressive ideas, where unusual partnerships can be formed between arts-focused developers, ambitious councils and engaged community groups. Architects are trained in facilitating discourse and working with community groups to make change possible.

Small-sites programmes create places and spaces of distinction, where design capitalises on existing character. The integration of historic buildings within regeneration schemes can create very popular destinations and act as a catalyst for further investment. The decision to retain or remove existing building fabric is a key consideration of these developments (eg. Hotwalls Studio in Portsmouth, or Wapping Wharf and Tobacco Factory in Bristol).

An architecture of re-use and adaptive repurposing is key in these projects. There are creative developments that integrate historic buildings, such as the likes of The Malings in Newcastle, York Central, Birmingham Library or Swindon's Carriage Works conversion. The following section is a selection of examples (cases) of urban regeneration where the strategies have been successfully applied, including the comparative dimension explaining the emergence of policy thinking around urban regeneration in the UK.

The selection includes interesting mixes of uses that amplify the uniqueness of buildings and place and that have often become an advantage of large-scale urban regeneration projects sitting side-by-side with smaller interventions.

The Selected Cases: What Makes These Places Unique?

The great post-industrial regions of the UK need greater appreciation from London and a greater distribution of wealth and support from the centre. While the post-war ambition was expressed in the development of new towns; today we appreciate and respect the careful densification, subtle stitching of building and place, and that the towns' rich industrial heritage plays a part in their resourceful regeneration. It is unbelievable that there are still plenty of areas in our towns and cities that are under-utilised where there is not yet enough intensity of activity. The robust British landscape still bears the scars of the old industries which are only slowly healing into the surrounding terrain.

Frequently, regional universities are the drivers of urban renewal, regenerating the towns and cities and their role cannot be underestimated. The campuses are frequently embedded in the city and create civic spaces and significant new buildings woven into the fabric and integrating historic buildings.

Interesting mixes of uses amplify the uniqueness of buildings and place and have often become an advantage to large-scale urban regeneration projects sitting side-by-side with smaller interventions. Local architects embrace the site-specific vernacular with skill and care, using locally sourced materials such as clay tiles, bricks, locally grown timber and flint which provide a sense of scale and locality.

The seismic retail change in our commercial centres, enforced by 'big box' architecture at the fringe and new online shopping habits ignores the sense of place and shopping experience in a walkable town centre. Instead, we can create a small-sites programme with places and spaces of distinction, where design capitalises on existing character. The integration of historic buildings with regeneration schemes can create very popular destinations and act as a catalyst for further investment. The decision to retain or remove existing building fabric is a key consideration of these developments.

Numerous architects facilitate discourse and work with community groups to make change. Architects often possess an ability to bring people and processes together, and combine tradition with progressive ideas, where unusual partnerships are forming between arts-focused developers and ambitious councils.

The Selected Cases (in order from South to North):

1 **Brighton & Hove**
New Road at Brighton's Cultural Mile as a place for people
2 **Hastings**
Hastings Pier redevelopment
3 **Portsmouth**
Hotwalls Studios: adaptive reuse of historical arches
4 **Bristol**
Wapping Wharf with Gaol Ferry Steps; Tobacco Factory and the Bristol is Open initiative
5 **Cardiff**
Cardiff Bay Waterfront with Roald Dahl Plass
6 **Ebbsfleet**
A new Garden City in North Kent
7 **Cambridge**
Eddington: a new compact neighbourhood as part of North West Cambridge
8 **Birmingham**
Birmingham Interchange (High Speed 2) Railway Station; and Birmingham Library and Centenary Square
9 **Liverpool**
Granby Four Streets in Toxteth: affordable housing
10 **Leeds**
South Bank: a landmark regeneration project in Leeds Centre and the Climate Innovation District.
11 **York**
York Central
12 **Newcastle upon Tyne**
The Malings on Ouseburn River
13 **Glasgow**
Glasgow City College's new City Campus

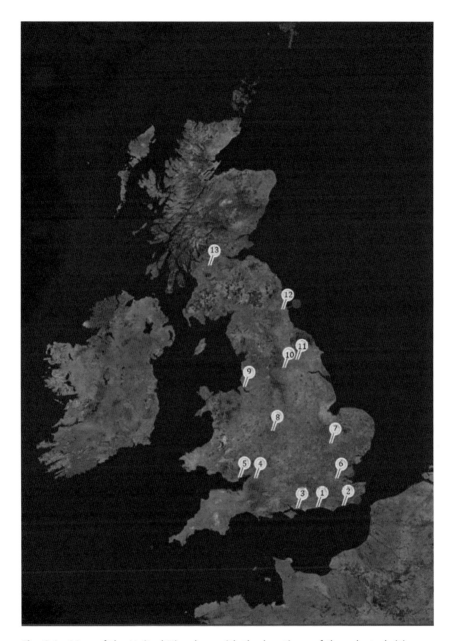

Fig. 6.1 Map of the United Kingdom with the locations of the selected cities

Brighton & Hove

New Road at Brighton's Cultural Mile as a Place for People (2010)

This project contributes to a high-quality public space network for a compact, walkable, mixed-use city, improving connectivity.

Brighton is the former royal seaside retreat and fashionable nineteenth-century bath town on the south coast of England, and the city still displays urban grandeur combined with a lively human scale. The Royal Pavilion, also known as the Brighton Pavilion, is a former royal residence located close to Marine Parade. Brighton became accessible to Londoners by rail in 1841, increasing its popularity with the masses. Multi-cultural Brighton & Hove attracts millions of visitors every year and New Road lies at the heart of Brighton's 'Cultural Mile' stretching from the pier to the popular North Laine neighbourhood. Brighton & Hove expects to grow by over 20,000 people between 2015 and 2030.

Pedestrianising streets is often controversial as people are concerned about the diverted flow of car traffic. However, numerous examples where streets have been pedestrianised have shown that it rarely creates any traffic problems, as the car traffic effectively 'vanishes'. Creating a walkable space is like curating the city; it is about high quality pavement materials, nice details and furnishing, and night-time illumination. Carefully designed lighting is a key to making people feel welcome and safe at night.

This new pedestrian space is located next to the Royal Pavilion and its gardens. It is part of a series of measures to reduce the importance of car use, while promoting accessibility and a high-quality walking experience. New Road had become a run-down and underperforming back alley that had developed into a hub of anti-social behaviour, failing to attract small businesses or visitors.

Today, New Road throngs with people, buskers, diners sitting at street cafes, cyclists and, strangest of all, cars. New Road today is not a pedestrianised street any more but a 'shared space' street, accommodating both vehicles and pedestrians.

The city council knew that this ideally located street had significant potential for upgrading and that it was not serving local residents or businesses well. In 2005 it was initially decided to close the street to all vehicles, but the designers convinced the council to create a new type of street: a shared space street where slow-moving cars are welcome, but on pedestrians' terms. As the street was to remain fully open to all types of traffic, the design of the surface played an important role in directing movement, and the street surface and furniture are laid out to encourage defensive driver behaviour. For the edges with adjoining streets, a heavy split-faced finish was used to generate a slight rumble strip that provides the motorist with a signal that they are entering a different type of space.

Before the design phase, significant time was spent to investigate the usage behaviour of the street and area to find out where people liked to enjoy the sun, how they informally used the space to relax, and how they moved through the space. The architects mapped pedestrian movement across the city and looked at the hierarchy of spaces and streets, coming to the conclusion that New Road could become a lively public space.

Paving, seating and lighting invite people into the space: Gehl Architects and Landscape Projects reimagined the street as a natural stone surface where rigid features like kerbs and crossings were removed, inviting pedestrians to move freely over the entire area, and giving pedestrians priority over all other users. The blend of colours and use of white granite kerbs laid flush with the surface all played a part in suggesting particular routes through the space, while physical barriers, such as upstand kerbs, were removed.

Along the edge of the Royal Gardens Park, a finely crafted, long wooden bench was placed that allows people to observe and look onto the active public space that has become a 'stage'. The fence to the garden curves in sections to become the extruded bench, with its geometry derived from armchairs and their more relaxed approach to sitting.

New Road looks like a space for people and car drivers recognise it and respect the pedestrians. It reopened in 2010 and quickly became very popular: traffic levels have dropped by over 90 percent and the number of pedestrians using the street has increased by over 60 percent. It is obvious that people enjoy being there and a recent survey indicated that 86 percent of residents would like to see more areas like New Road in Brighton.

The more pedestrian-friendly approach in the public realm has paid off numerous times. It improves connectivity and links the Royal Pavilion gardens to the new library. The improved quality of the street made social interaction possible and changed the dynamic of the street, generating a new urban culture. New Road has become one of the most popular places to spend time in Brighton & Hove and this relatively small project has helped to transform the entire area into a 'Cultural Quarter', which is now contributing to the city's thriving economy.

This regeneration project shows that street life can be created if spaces are well designed. New Road is an example that, if we give back streets to the pedestrian, public life will return to the city. The project relates to Strategy 2: Developing and renewing the public space network for a compact, walkable and mixed-use city.

Figs. 6.2 and 6.3   New Road in Brighton

Hastings

Hastings Pier Redevelopment (2016)

This project contributes to transforming the waterfront of a resilient, future-proof coastal city by reusing an existing structure.

Hastings is an English town on the southeast coast best known for the 1066 Battle of Hastings; the Norman ruins of Hastings Castle, once home to William the Conqueror, overlook the English Channel. Like many coastal towns, the population of Hastings grew significantly as a result of the construction of railway links to London and the fashionable growth of seaside holidays during the Victorian era. Sea air was discovered to be particularly beneficial for health and seaside towns transformed into poplar resorts for early mass tourism. Today Hastings has a population of 90,000 people.

Regeneration programmes have lifted the area along the seafront promenade, which is now seeing a boost in tourism, economy and enterprises—and the redeveloped pier plays a significant part in the town's renaissance. Hastings Pier represents a new beginning for the town.

The historic pier, first built in 1870, reopened to the public in 2016 after a £14 million restoration, partly crowdfunded. The 280 metre long Victorian pier featured in its heyday a 2000-seat pavilion, a shooting range, slot machines and 'animated pictures'. But it fell into disrepair and was closed in 2008 for safety reasons. In 2010 a devastating fire tore through the pier, ravaging 95 percent of the upper structure. The fire prompted a local action group to launch a campaign to raise funds to renovate the site, which also benefited from the Heritage Lottery Fund. A charity was set up in 2011 to take ownership of the pier and commission its redevelopment.

The pleasure pier is a distinctly British phenomenon, with the first recorded structure opened in 1814 on the Isle of Wight. The redevelopment of Hastings Pier includes a new bar and restaurant in the pavilion building. The new pier is designed as an enormous, free, public, multi-purpose platform over the sea—inspiring temporary installations and events across a variety of scales.

Pier redevelopment project won the prestigious 2017 Stirling Prize and the judges commented: "This project shows that local communities working with architects can make a huge difference. Councils should take inspiration from Hastings Pier, and open their eyes to the unique assets that can be created when such collaborations take place."

dRMM Architects noted that the fire presented an opportunity to give the pier a new future. "There was no sense in trying to reconstruct it as a 19th century pier—that typology had gone with the fire. There was an opportunity to reuse and reinvent the pier and give it a new future," he said (2017). Establishing a new role for pleasure piers in the twenty-first century as a contemporary multi-purpose space was invented earlier in Southend, but at Hastings Pier, the architects provided a blueprint for how existing piers can be reimagined. The project has been dealt with in two parts: the original ironwork column and truss structure, and the deck above with its two timber pavilions. The architects and engineers carefully surveyed what remained after the fire, kept what was salvageable and replaced what was not with contemporary versions. A small new visitor centre and café with large windows is clad with reclaimed timber salvaged from the fire and offers a roof top viewing terrace providing magnificent views out across the Channel. The vast pier deck offers an uninterrupted flexible space for markets, large-scale concerts and public gatherings. This relates to Strategy 6: Using new public space as a catalyst for a better city.

A national treasure brought back to life as a flexible well-serviced platform able to accommodate a broad range of community and commercial uses. The architects' conceptual basis for the re-design of the pier was not to create the predictable (and unnecessary) 'hero' building, but instead providing open space to allow universal access for an endless range of future possibilities. The Pier is an extension of the promenade from which it projects—a public, open space that allows the experience of being surrounded by sea and 'walking on water'. The new Pier has become a catalyst for the urban regeneration of Hastings.

Figs. 6.4–6.7   Hastings Pier redevelopment

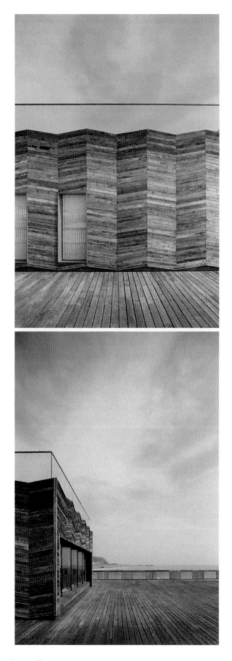

Figs. 6.4–6.7   (continued)

Portsmouth

Hotwalls Studios: The Adaptive Reuse of Historical Arches (2016)

This project contributes to urban culture and heritage—maintaining a unique sense of place through cultural refurbishment.

The *Hotwalls Studios* brings artists and designer-makers together in 13 working studios in an exceptional heritage location in Old Portsmouth. Located at Point Battery, between the historical Square and Round Towers, it has seen the transformation of former fifteenth century military barracks and brick arches into artist studios and a café. The sea defences were originally constructed in the 1420s and were rebuilt during Elizabeth I's reign. As well as defending Portsmouth against attack, over time the arches in the walls below the Round Tower have been used for arts and craft exhibitions for local visitors and tourists.

There are many theories as to why the area is known as the Hotwalls but its association with artists dates back to the 1960s and 70s when artists began selling paintings from the open arches at Point Battery. This has provided inspiration for the Hotwalls Studios project and Portsmouth's flourishing creative sector.

The modest £2m development received government funding via the Coastal Communities Fund. It is a good example for the benefits from smaller impactful projects. Rather than pursuing one large vanity project, cities can be much more effectively regenerated by instead investing in ten smaller projects at different locations, a strategy that Jaime Lerner called 'Urban Acupuncture'.

In 2011 the Seafront Strategy set out the idea of transforming the area adjacent to the Round Tower into a vibrant arts and crafts quarter. Following extensive public consultation the plans were adopted by council in 2012. A new triangular public square with high-quality pavement and trees along the street are the centre piece. The vacant arches, accessed directly from this square, were converted into artist studio space. The project creates new jobs and supports the emerging creative industries. Artists who take up one of the new studios enjoy a unique opportunity to show-case their work to the public and also benefit from the potential for exhibitions in the recently refurbished Round Tower.

Hotwalls revives the historic brick arches and introduces an enhanced public space. The artist studios are offered at a lower rent for new start-up businesses. The 13 studios have been created for both new and established artists, they vary in size and there is an opportunity to share spaces. With completely glazed fronts, the studios aren't for shy and retiring artist types as the new creative quarter attracts large numbers of visitors to the area. Artists are selling their works direct to customers from their studios.

The Studios have emerged as the focus for a cohesive, consistent, high quality, creative 'offer', acting as a platform to showcase creative organisations, artists, makers and their networks.

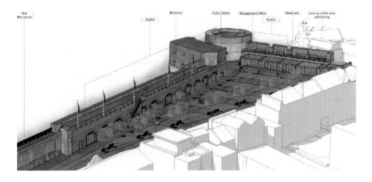

Figs. 6.8–6.13   Hotwalls Studios in Old Portsmouth

Figs. 6.8–6.13   (continued)

Figs. 6.8–6.13 (continued)

Bristol

Wapping Wharf with Gaol Ferry Steps; Tobacco Factory and the Bristol Is Open Initiative

These projects in Bristol contribute to the vision of a vibrant, regenerated and smart city, as supported by *Bristol is Open*.

The city of Bristol has taken the challenge of sustainable regeneration very seriously and there is a long tradition of municipal leadership and political activism. As a result, Bristol has been remarkably successful in developing regenerated places to live and work, such as Harbourside, Paintworks and Wapping Wharf.

Bristol has an urban population of around 600,000 people, making it England's sixth-most populous city. With a highly skilled workforce drawn from its universities, Bristol claims to have the largest cluster of IT experts and computer chip manufacturers outside of Silicon Valley.

In the past, Bristol docks was an important area with shipbuilding and warehouses right in the centre of the city. However, since the 1970s, Bristol's dockland areas went into decline following the arrival of large cargo ships that could no longer navigate the Avon River. This prompted the closure of several industries around the docks such as the tobacco factories, sand dredging industries and lead-shot works, which left several buildings empty and sites derelict. In the 1980s, unemployment and poverty levels in Bristol were amongst the highest in the country. The area near Temple Meads Station was one that had suffered particularly badly from the closures. In addition, as the docks declined, Bristol was faced with several problems, such as growing social and economic inequalities, vast areas of derelict land and high unemployment. As a consequence, the Urban Development Corporation (UDC) was set up to regenerate the inner city areas by attracting private investment to the worst areas. They could purchase any necessary land and then had to stimulate the economy to attract private investment. For instance the UDC purchased a 900-acre inner-city site in an area of industrial decline with the objective to improve the existing infrastructure, make sure there was sufficient housing, and attract new industries—providing jobs and investment. One major criticism against the UDC is that very little funding went into environmental improvements, training or social facilities.

Beginning of the 1980s, the Georgian-era plazas Queen Square and Portland Square were restored and the Broadmead shopping area regenerated. The relocation of the Avonmouth Docks and Royal Portbury Dock around 10 km downstream from the city centre allowed for the redevelopment of the old dock area. Although the docks were seen as derelict industrial sites of little value, the inaugural 1996 *International Festival of the Sea* held in the docks was important as it affirmed the area as a potential leisure asset.

The docklands redevelopment has been financed by a mixture of public and private money with the overall aim of providing a new creative quarter with a mix of leisure facilities, housing and offices. It has received substantial funding from the national lottery. Over the past thirty years, the area has undergone major changes culminating in the opening of the new IMAX theatre, at-Bristol science museum and Millennium Square. The area is now one of the largest redevelopment projects in Europe, with ongoing development as proposals are made for the redevelopment of other sites.

More recently (2018), the city of Bristol has engaged in extensive consultation for urban living in higher densities to use land more efficiently (published in the Urban Living SPD draft document), which contains a number of policies to facilitate infill development at higher densities and compile lessons learnt from other high density development. It defines the areas considered suitable for higher density development (such as transport hubs), and gives design guidance on how to better integrate high density into the wider neighbourhoods. Interestingly, it was agreed that density should not be the sole defining measure of assessment, as focus should be on design quality and integration into an area.

Tobacco Factory in Bedminster, a series of large empty red-brick factories built around 1910, has developed into a trendy theatre venue and regenerated complex in Bristol's lively Southville area. In 1993, local architect George Ferguson bought one of the few remaining factories on Raleigh Road to save the great red brick complex from demolition. At this time, his plan to redevelop it as a creative, mixed-use community building was met by developers with widespread bemusement. North Street, Ashton and Bedminster, not long ago on its knees, is now one of the liveliest independent high streets and neighbourhoods in Bristol. The lesson is to make the most of what is already there and inject new life into old structures and places to create socially and culturally vibrant communities.

Social diversity has played a major part in shaping the special social profile of these developments. Less so at *Wapping Wharf*, which is a trendy waterfront development: a residential and retail quarter leading from south Bristol to the public waterfront and Millennium Square, featuring over 600 upmarket new homes, mainly small apartments. The developers of Wapping Wharf have worked very cleverly with local independent businesses to create a new retail street to the South of the historic docks: Gaol Ferry Steps. Wapping Wharf is also the location of CARGO, a retail yard made of converted shipping containers (based on the earlier success of BOXPARK in London Shhoreditch). Based on land that was previously derelict, Wapping Wharf has restored several key listed buildings and the Old City Gaol gatehouse.

Bristol Is Open is an initiative with a focus on smart citizens, smart energy and citizen participation by using digital tools online. This smart city research network platform helps Bristol lead the way in the UK in areas such as citizen-centric open data access, energy innovation and community engagement.

The platform allows local companies and start-ups to work with *Bristol Is Open* to trial their latest technologies and apps. This relates to Strategy 10: Cities benefitting from a new shared knowledge platform.

Fig. 6.14   Tobacco Factory in Bristol Southville

Figs. 6.15–6.19   Bristol Wapping Wharf with Gaol Ferry Steps

Figs. 6.15–6.19   (continued)

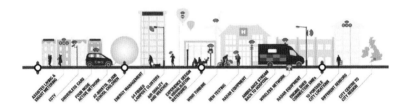

Fig. 6.20   Graph of *Bristol Is Open*

Cardiff

Cardiff Bay Waterfront with Roald Dahl Plass (2002)

This project contributes to the creation of a new waterfront plaza and includes an innovative approach to the management of this vibrant public space.

Cardiff is a port city on the south coast of Wales, where the River Taff meets the Severn Estuary. The city of Cardiff was proclaimed as the capital city of Wales in 1955. It is the eleventh-largest city in the United Kingdom, with a population of around 380,000. A small town until the early nineteenth century, Cardiff's major port for the transport of coal contributed to its prominence and rise as a major city.

Roald Dahl Plass is a public space located in Cardiff Bay south of the city centre, named after Cardiff-born author Roald Dahl. The square is home to the Welsh National Assembly building (by Richard Rogers) and next to the Wales Millennium Centre, a new performing arts centre. The bowl-like shape of the space has made it a popular amphitheatre for hosting open-air events and concerts.

The area was once part of a thriving coal port during the latter half of the nineteenth century and the first half of the twentieth century. The dock opened in 1839 and was over 1200 metres long, allowing up to 300 vessels to berth at any time. Around 1910, Cardiff had become the largest exporter of coal in the world, exporting over 10 million tonnes of coal per year.

However following World War II, the Welsh coal mining industry collapsed, with the last coal export through the dock taking place in 1964. Subsequently, the dock was filled in to prevent collapse of the surrounding walls. The area entered a period of decay and dereliction until the 1980s, when the Cardiff Bay area was regenerated. 'Plass' is the Norwegian word for 'Place' or 'Square', as both of Dahl's parents were from Norway. At the north end of the Plass is the Water Tower, which stands at approximately 21 m high. The historic remnants of the dock basin and red brick of the imposing Pierhead Building firmly root the location with its historic past, creating a unique urban setting.

Cardiff has several regeneration projects such as the Cardiff Bay Waterfront, the St. David's 2 Centre and the International Sports Village in Cardiff Bay which played a part in the London 2012 Olympics.

The Cardiff Bay Development Corporation acted as a major driver for the Bay area's regeneration and unlocking potential for new leisure, residential and employment opportunities. The corporation took some important early steps, promoting the tunnelling of the docklands relief road beneath Roald Dahl Plass. This decision to sink the relief road beneath the plaza showed foresight, allowing the city and its pedestrian plaza to be reunited with the waterfront, creating a high quality pedestrian environment.

There is a strong emphasis on the area's seafront location, reviving the contact that the city had with the sea (the Bristol Channel) over hundreds of years. The project provides a unique waterfront setting befitting a seat of government and national institutions, and the Roald Dahl Plass (designed by Nicolas Hare Architects) has defined the ambition that goes with this, through the creation of a national gathering place. It offers a large, multi-purpose urban civic space that was previously absent in the city.

The Academy of Urbanism notes (2018): 'Despite the nature of the place being highly inclusive and accessible, the area still feels disconnected from Cardiff city centre. Measures to improve the connectivity of the area, particularly as part of a light-rail system could further allow the area to flourish in the longer term and assist with its ongoing regeneration.'

Figs. 6.21–6.23   The Roald Dahl Plaza in Cardiff

Figs. 6.21–6.23 (continued)

Ebbsfleet

A New Garden City in North Kent (2030)

This project contributes to high-quality architectural design and public space in an entire new town as a catalyst for a better city. This project is not strictly regeneration but rather new development within a context that will be regenerated.

The guiding principle is to develop the project at relatively high density in order to support high quality public space and easy access to public transport (including Ebbsfleet International, the railway link with the EuroStar train between London and Paris). When completed, the whole quarter has the potential to become a model for urban sustainability and regeneration of a region through the construction of a twenty-first century new town. This will be one of the UK Government's 10 Healthy New Towns for an ageing population that will get developed across England. *Ebbsfleet Garden City* is the largest of the pilots and aims to promote health, wellbeing and radically rethink delivery of health and care services (called 'integrated care').

The Ebbsfleet Development Corporation was established by the government to speed up delivery of up to 15,000 homes, 30,000 new jobs and create a twenty-first century Garden City. The shared vision and masterplan phase has been approved in 2018, and Ebbsfleet Garden City has received £275 million to deliver all of the infrastructure required.

The Grove Road and Northfleet Riverside locations, once solely locations for heavy industry, will be transformed into 980 new homes (up to a third will be affordable housing), providing residents with better access to the Thames riverfront and include new open spaces. Six simple design principles have been developed:

* Develop stronger links between the existing and the new communities.
* Create a healthy, safe and secure environment for all.
* Respect local history and character.
* Provide a mix of housing types and tenures.
* Give as many people as possible a river view.
* Create links to help access the river and High Street.

The masterplan for this new town has a clearly identifiable centre within a mixed-use neighbourhood and green fingers in between. It is not conceived as an assemblage of separate villages. In the first phase there will be 5000 homes to be completed by 2021. The Swanscombe area is defined as the major employment source and as commercial hub.

Ebbsfleet Garden City is another good example of the powerful role of new infrastructure and railway stations to create a platform of wider urban change (similar to the current plans at Birmingham Interchange or Leeds South Bank).

Figs. 6.24–6.27   Ebbsfleet Garden City, the masterplan and Grove Road and Northfleet Riverside projects

Figs. 6.24–6.27 (continued)

Cambridge

Eddington: A New Compact Neighbourhood, Part of the North West Cambridge Development (2017)

This project contributes to inclusive, mixed-used, low-carbon urban living.

Cambridge is a key university city on the River Cam, founded in the twelfth century (the University of Cambridge was founded in 1209). Cambridge is located approximately 80 km north of London and its population is around 130,000 (including 25,000 students).

Eddington is Cambridge's new exemplary sustainable community that will grow step-by-step until 2027, providing in phase one in total over 3000 homes and student residences and 100,000 sqm of commercial space. The compact development on the 150-hectare site discourages the use and ownership of cars, while a total of 12,000 bike spaces will be provided for the 8500 residents and an excellent range of public transport is available. Master planner WilkinsonEyre notes: 'Three-storey townhouses as 'walk-ups' and five-story apartment buildings are combined with a diverse mix of uses throughout the area, served by a central CHP energy centre.'

Every new resident has a meeting with a travel planner who advises on alternatives to driving, and there is only one parking space for every five flats, reserved for university staff who will occupy half of the 3000 homes. This means that most homes don't need a driveway and visitors arriving by car will have to pay for parking if they stay more than 90 minutes. Relatively few residents own a car and there is a popular car sharing scheme.

The idea of the new quarter is the 'city of short distances' where everything one might regularly need is close at hand. Cyclists and pedestrians (not cars) have the shortest and most direct access to the city centre. The very low car ownership has helped to build a sense of community and people are keener to do things together. Cycling has been made more popular and efficient so that almost 20 percent of all trips to work are now made by bike. This has been achieved by a combination of measures, including an extensive network of cycle lanes and safe bicycle storage facilities. There is much good planning, for instance, the flexible ground floor units for commercial, retail or community uses are lining the new pedestrian routes to activate the public realm.

There is also plenty of integrated technology: The new neighbourhood has district heating and hot water supply so none of the homes needs its own boiler. Waste management is also innovative: wheelie bins are banned and waste is disposed of through chutes leading to underground chambers equipped with sensors telling the waste company when they need emptying.

Eddington has the UK's largest rainwater recycling system, with a network of bio-filtration swales in the landscape draining into newly excavated lakes. Water is naturally filtered through reed beds and pumped back as grey water for irrigation, use in washing machines or to flush toilets. This results in extremely reduced water consumption, which is only half the UK average of 150 litres per day. Two newly created public parks cover more than 80 acres, helping to make walking and cycling more pleasant.

Figs. 6.28–6.31 Eddington, a new urban living quarter in North West Cambridge

Figs. 6.28–6.31   (continued)

Figs. 6.32–6.34   Images of built Eddington, a new urban living quarter in North West Cambridge

Birmingham

Birmingham Interchange (High Speed 2) Railway Station (2026); and Birmingham Library and Centenary Square (2014)

This project contributes to cities sharing their experiences, learning from each other by exchanging experiences and best practice.

Birmingham is a city in the West Midlands with an estimated population of over 1.1 million people from very different backgrounds, making it the second most populous city in both England and the United Kingdom as a whole (after London). Birmingham has a truly cosmopolitan and multi-cultural quality and is progressing an ongoing programme to regenerate the city centre, which includes its extensive system of canals.

The historic waterway network that was once its crowning glory has been regenerated since the mid-1990s, and around Brindleyplace, a typical inner-city brownfield site, the canal-side location for the new Symphony Hall and the International Convention Centre emerged.

Having risen from the doldrums of the recession, it now draws in over 10,000 visitors a day, with events including the popular Dragonboat Festival, live music in The Water's Edge bandstand and in Oozells Square, and festivals of film and food. Other towns like Walsall are following suit with smaller scale waterside developments of their own. Over 1200 homes will be built at the derelict canal-side Port Loop, at Edgbaston Reservoir, as an urban neighbourhood with terraced houses at a density of 120 dwellings per hectare, integrating the former Tube Works factory (developed by Urban Splash and Places for People).

Birmingham Interchange is the new High Speed 2 (HS2) *Parkway* railway station in the Borough of Solihull (close to Birmingham Airport and 10 km from Birmingham Centre), expected to open in 2026. It is the key part in the development of a new town called *The Hub* around this node of crucial transport infrastructure. In 2017, a Growth and Infrastructure Plan for *The Hub* area was developed by the Urban Growth Company, with the HS2 Interchange Station at its heart. This masterplan outlines the opportunity to create up to 77,000 new jobs, 775,000 square metres of new commercial space and 4000 homes. It is a strong first step in ensuring that the masterplan, together with the aspirations of other neighbouring stakeholders, can be delivered within a coherent framework for infrastructure delivery. The scale of the project is immense: the arrival of HS2 at Arden Cross presents significant opportunities for the development of a new urban centre that champions the integration of the natural environment with economic growth. This project is not strictly regeneration but rather new development within a context that, as a consequence, will be regenerated.

Birmingham Library is a flagship urban regeneration project for the city's redevelopment and a good example how one large cultural project can become the catalyst for urban regeneration for an entire city. Located on Centenary Square, it is at the heart of an area that has constantly evolved and adapted since the 1700s, from housing to canals to industry, and more recently, to open public space.

The new library has been an impressive success with the local community, densifying uses as a means of strengthening the community. Since its opening in 2013, borrowing and visitor numbers at the new Library of Birmingham are double those of its predecessor building. The £190m building, which has over a million books (it is Europe's largest public library), was built to replace the old Central Library, which was since demolished.

Sandwiched between a 1930s building and a 1960s theatre, the new Library of Birmingham fronts one of three piazzas that comprises Centenary Square. The building is made up of a stack of four rectangular volumes, which are staggered to create various canopies and terraces. The lowest level extends out beneath Centenary Square, where the architects have created a sunken circular courtyard that functions as an informal amphitheatre.

The library itself was conceived as a public space. 'We needed many ground floors,' explained Francine Houben of Mecanoo Architects, 'so we introduced a ground floor, a mezzanine, a mid-lower ground floor and a mid-mid-lower ground floor in the form of gently descending terraces.'

Figs. 6.35 and 6.36 Aerial photo of Birmingham Brindleyplace urban regeneration. Section of the new library and square

Figs. 6.37–6.39 Birmingham Interchange planned new town called The Hub

Figs. 6.37–6.39 (continued)

Figs. 6.40–6.42 Birmingham Library and Centenary Square

Figs. 6.40–6.42 (continued)

Liverpool

Affordable Housing at Granby 4 Streets in Toxteth (2005–2015)

This project contributes to urban culture and heritage—maintaining a unique sense of place while providing affordable housing solutions that avoid or minimise gentrification.

Liverpool is a maritime city in northwest England, located where the River Mersey meets the Irish Sea. It was a key trade and migration port from the 18th to the early 20th centuries, and the city has been an economic dynamo for the country throughout the nineteenth century. Today, its estimated population is around 500,000 people (2017), and its metropolitan area is the fifth-largest in the UK, with a population of around 2.25 million people.

In the 1950s and 60s, significant rebuilding followed the war, including massive housing estates. Much of the immediate reconstruction of the city centre has been deeply unpopular. The region and city of Liverpool suffered massive deindustrialisation with the shipyards and textile industries closing down in the 1970s and 80s. As a consequence, the city has to completely rethink its economic role and spatial structure.

Much of Liverpool's city centre dates from the early eighteenth century, with some grand buildings along the Mersey River waterfront, where the iconic mercantile buildings known as the 'Three Graces' stand on the Pier Head. As a major British port, the docks in Liverpool have historically always been central to the city's development. Overall the city is relatively compact and easy to get around. Spearheaded by the massive Liverpool ONE development (a retail and business development with luxury apartments, completed in 2008), urban regeneration is ongoing as projects find investors.

However, very little social or affordable housing has been built since 2005 in part because of high land value. Affordable housing is essential because it creates social diversity and helps to reduce gentrification. Granby 4 Streets (initiated by Assemble Architects) has been praised for its careful incremental approach: Assemble worked closely with the Granby 4 Streets Community Land Trust to refurbish ten derelict Victorian terraced houses, supporting a 20 year battle by local residents to save the houses from demolition.

Granby 4 Streets in Toxteth was once a lively high street at the centre of Liverpool's most racially and ethnically diverse community. The demolition of all but four of Granby's streets of terraces during decades of 'urban renewal' initiatives saw a once thriving community of 68 houses scattered, and left the remaining four households of 'Granby 4 Streets' sparsely located, interspersed with boarded up houses. Over twenty years, families had been moved out by housing associations, their homes tinned up and the bricks painted black.

Assemble wrote: 'This is a bottom-up example of how urban residents can successfully influence change in their own community. The resourceful, creative actions of the group were fundamental to finally bringing these streets out of dereliction and back into use. Over two decades they cleared, planted, painted, and campaigned in order to reclaim their street and maximise the potential of existing buildings.'

In 2011 the group of residents entered into an innovative form of community land ownership, the *Granby 4 Streets Community Land Trust*, with the intention of bringing the empty homes back into use as affordable housing. Assemble Architects worked closely with the Trust and others to present a sustainable and incremental vision for the area that built on the hard work already done by local residents and translated it to the refurbishment of housing, public space and the provision of new job opportunities.

The group of activists beat a housing system that failed their community and then judged that community a failure. Their overall approach is characterised by celebrating the value of the area's architectural and cultural heritage, supporting public involvement and partnership working, offering local skills training and employment opportunities, and nurturing the resourcefulness and DIY spirit that defines the four streets.

Figs. 6.43–6.48   The Granby 4 Streets estate, before and after renovation

Figs. 6.43–6.48 (continued)

Leeds

South Bank: A Landmark Regeneration Project in Leeds Centre; and the Climate Innovation District

These projects will contribute to high-quality architectural design and public space as a catalyst for a better city.

The city of Leeds, situated on the River Aire in West Yorkshire, has a population of around 750,000 people and has recently experienced strong growth in population. The urban strategy for regenerating the city include ideas to develop brownfield sites as dense and concentrated neighbourhoods, to result in a greater diversity of housing designs and concepts, with older buildings being preserved and reused.

A grand vision for the *South Bank Leeds* regeneration project has been launched in 2016, which will double the size of the city centre and include parks, public spaces, a rejuvenated waterfront and new entrance to Leeds Railway Station. It plans to restore historic buildings and include an educational district that will cater for 10,000 students. The ambitious vision plans to complement what the city already has, not to repeat it, and includes new residential, commercial and leisure developments alongside major improvements to the public realm. It also plans for a new city park that will host major events and activities, a health-focused area with outdoor gym equipment, and a series of smaller, intimate green spaces and urban allotment gardens. It will have at least six new public spaces along the waterfront, putting the river at the heart, and inspiring people to enjoy the waterfront in new ways. The regeneration of South Bank Leeds is expected to create 35,000 new jobs and 4000 new homes.

The new High Speed 2 (HS2) station forecourt will be accompanied by a gateway space that leads straight down to the river from station, and a redesigned stretch of the waterfront east of the station that could include a bridge between Sovereign Square and the new park, prioritising pedestrians and cyclists. The plan will put a host of historic buildings back into use, including iconic buildings like Hunslet Mill and Victoria Works that are currently empty. It is envisaged that HS2 is also going to be game changer for Leeds (numerous cities in the UK have based their regeneration plans on the HS2 transport investment, including Birmingham and York). These cities expect that they will become more accessible and that HS2 will give businesses in the north a boost, as well as driving future tourism.

Leeds City Council have fought to combine the new HS2 station with the existing one, as a unified space with restaurants and shops, and surrounded by well-positioned bus stops, taxi points and car parks to help travellers continue their journey. The aim here is to use the station as a catalyst for the urban regeneration of the entire centre, attracting more landmark developments and community services to the area, as King's Cross & St Pancras did in London. The plan makes pedestrians and cyclists a priority, planning to improve the experience for cyclists and pedestrians. That means extending and enhancing the existing pedestrianised space into the South Bank and building new cycle lanes, to create a new City Boulevard that will stretch from the Headrow, past the waterfront and the new Leeds Station, all the way down to the junction between Victoria Road and Meadow Lane.

The plan includes measures to narrow existing streets, and car traffic will be encouraged to move around the city centre rather than through it, by expanding the City Loop. This will be accompanied by the new parking strategy which will place Park and Ride stations outside the Inner Ring Road, long stay parking outside the new City Boulevard, and a mix of short stay and strategic long stay parking in the centre itself. It is expected that the result will be a safer, more accessible city centre, with easy routes into and around Leeds.

The *Climate Innovation District* (CID) in Leeds is a mixed use project that aims to radically reduce the carbon footprint of its residents by over 50 percent. Swedish master planners White Arkitekter noted: "Designed to reduce carbon emissions throughout, the Climate Innovation District is underpinned by good design and great places. In addition to low-carbon homes and a landscape that uses ecosystem services, its city centre location allows for walking and cycling, improving air quality and reducing emissions."

The CID masterplan develops a central brownfield site on the river and converts it into a mixed-use sustainable neighbourhood of more than 500 apartments and homes. With a high standard of environmental performance (the energy-efficient homes will be timber structures to *Passivhaus* standard, with solar panels and green roofs) and fully integrated services including healthcare, commercial offices and manufacturing, the new quarter will offer a diversity of green spaces to encourage social interaction and physical activity. Ensuring the quarter is pedestrian and cycle-friendly, non-vehicular movement is a priority and careful consideration was given to the distance people will have to walk to access daily facilities. A mix of small and large homes (many located directly along the waterfront) will all be manufactured on-site at the developer's prefab factory, which once under operation will be able to produce up to 750 low-carbon homes each year for future developments; including manufactured 8-storey timber buildings using massive timber construction.

Fig. 6.49   Leeds South Bank masterplan by Ian Simpson, 2014

Figs. 6.50–6.52 Leeds Climate Innovation District

York

York Central (2030)

This project is the largest regeneration project in the city's history and it will contribute to high-quality architectural design and public space as a catalyst for a better city.

The city of York in Yorkshire, northeast England, is a walled city founded by the Romans in 71 AD; it has a population of around 200,000 people. In the nineteenth century, York became a hub of the railway network and a confectionery manufacturing centre, but today, the economy of York is dominated by services, knowledge and tourism.

York Central is based on thinking long-term and making the most of what is already there. The long-neglected area of land behind the railway station features disused infrastructure and is York's largest brownfield site. Together with Network Rail, the National Railway Museum and The Homes and Communities Agency, the City of York Council is drawing up a new vision for the 178 acre site.

The redevelopment of York Central, also called the 'King's Cross of the North' will deliver major growth and enable the city to attract high value jobs, thousands of much needed energy-efficient homes and create world-class public spaces. This reduces the pressure to build on York's greenbelt. Local residents are involved in every step through a full public consultation process.

Some parts of the area were restricted to rail uses for more than 150 years. In 2016, the 45 hectare site was designated as a UK Government 'Housing Zone' and has also been awarded 'Enterprise Zone' status, which offers commercial occupiers significant incentives. It is hoped that *York Central* will power the city's economy into the future, helping to provide the homes the city needs and grow its economy by 20 per cent. The new vision could provide up to 120,000 sqm of high-quality office and retail space, a new hotel, create 6500 new jobs and 2500 new homes. Over the next 10 years, it will become the city's most attractive redevelopment area, also expanding the National Railway Museum.

To properly connect *York Central* to the existing City Gate and neighbouring communities, a new foot and cycling network will be created with a pedestrian and cycling bridge over the East Coast Mainline, bridging heavy infrastructural corridors. A new cycling highway will be linked up with public transport and the railway station.

The urban vision of master planners Allies & Morrison (with Arup) is centred on social inclusiveness and the belief that ordinary people should be able to benefit from urban development and be able to live close to public transport. The area will be developed incrementally, starting where it is easiest, and to make small site parcels available in phases. It is understood that York Central will only really begin to work when residents take a lead on the transformation too. This relates to Strategy 8: Thinking long-term and making the most of what we already have. Existing buildings will be maintained as much as possible and integrated, adaptively reused. The National Railway Museum will be a key anchor for homes and businesses coming to the site.

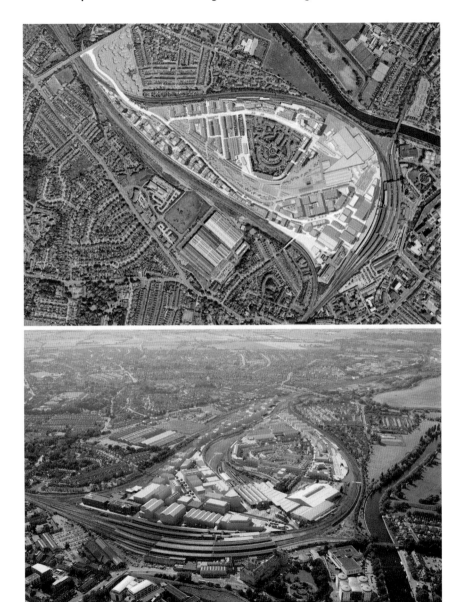

Figs. 6.53–6.57   York Central development

Figs. 6.53–6.57   (continued)

Newcastle upon Tyne

The Malings Housing Development on Ouseburn River (2015)

This project creates a sense of community and contributes to inclusive mixed-used urban living in the revitalised centre, minimising the need to drive by car.

The City of Newcastle in the northeast of England is a historic university city and a centre for the arts and sciences, with a population of around 300,000 people. A significant and innovative housing development in Newcastle is the *Byker Wall* designed by Ralph Erskine in 1970 (see Fig. 3.12).

The *Tyneside Flat* was the dominant nineteenth century housing form constructed at the time when the industrial centres on Tyneside were growing most rapidly. They can still be found in some areas in Newcastle but once dominated the streetscape on both sides of the Tyne. Tyneside flats were built as terraces, one of each pair of doors led to an upstairs flat while the other led into the ground-floor flat, each of two or three rooms. *The Malings*, a new development in the Ouseburn valley has recreated this typology; the architects were attracted by the possibilities of high density without building high and getting rid of common areas. The guiding idea of The Malings project was to develop the canal-side at high density in order to support a sustainable car-free lifestyle and to make the most of the waterside location. It is part of an overall drive to transform this former cradle of industry into a trendy cultural quarter and place for live bands, and The Malings are some of the first homes in this area for more than 60 years.

Situated half a mile downstream of Newcastle city centre, adjacent to the Quayside and named after the Malings Pottery dating back to 1817, the scheme comprises 76 low energy and eco-friendly homes on a 0.6ha site, with commercial units for local business and community uses that have completely transformed this characterful urban area. The innovative £16 million development at the heart of Newcastle's cultural quarter was designed by architects Ash Sakula. The dense street-based masterplan provides every occupant with their own front door, which creates a relationship to the street that positively connects residents to the place and each other. The materiality of The Malings is conventional locally-made red brick matched with timber details.

The plans carefully re-think the traditional *Tyneside Flat* housing typology and create a series of bespoke interlocking houses and apartments in a configuration that delivers strong views to context and private external space to all residents. The diversity of housing types includes stacked duplexes, detached tower houses and the use of large rooftop terraces and small courtyards, whereby each space opens towards the river (and new riverside walk). Each home feels as it has been individually designed, with its own unique plan. Organised in five fan-shaped fingers on the sloping site, the building blocks radiate out from the back of the site, stretching over sixty metres in length, with communal gardens, allotments, alleyways and a shared 'village square' in between. It resembles a medieval town where homes overlap and lock together; the achieved density of 137 homes per hectare gives this well-planned place character and has created a sought-after location.

Figs. 6.58–6.63 The romantic riverside setting of The Malings in Newcastle upon Tyne

Figs. 6.58–6.63   (continued)

Glasgow

Glasgow City College Has Inserted a New City Campus (2016)

This project contributes to the development of a vibrant university quarter as the regenerated and rejuvenated heart of the city.

Universities all over the UK develop vibrant quarters and make significant contributions to the regeneration of our cities through good architecture, walkable public space and strong pedestrian connectivity, which helps to integrate these compact and car-free new campus developments into their surrounding communities. Newcastle City Campus and Lincoln University Campus are good examples for patronage by universities for architectural excellence and the transformation of the city led by a higher education institution.

Fig. 6.64 New campus of the University of Lincoln

The city of Glasgow is a port city on the River Clyde in Scotland's western Lowlands, known for its Victorian and art nouveau architecture. Today Glasgow is a national cultural hub, home to institutions including the Scottish Opera, as well as acclaimed museums and universities. The city has one of the highest densities of any locality in Scotland at approximately 4000 people per sqkm. The city population is over 600,000 people. Comprehensive urban renewal projects in the 1960s and 70s resulted in large-scale relocation of people to designated new towns which reduced the population density.

Glasgow's new *City Campus* (for the City of Glasgow College) creates a sense of civic and knits together formerly neglected and fragmented parts of the city's northern edge. Consisting of over 60,000 sqm of floor area, the large building is located on a hill at the edge of the urban grid; its elevated location resembles an acropolis, and within Glasgow's eclectic mix of architectural styles (a rich legacy of the city's eighteenth to twentieth-century prosperity due to trade and shipbuilding), the idea of an acropolis is not alien. In fact, the large volume is well inserted in its urban and social context, which shows that even a large programme as this one can be sensitively integrated. It also creates good public space and pedestrian connectivity, as it offers a new public route through the project that links back the housing estate on one side to the city centre on the other side. The circulation is clearly organised: two large civic staircases are located externally and internally (in the large atrium described by the architects as a 'grand room'), which form the main pedestrian routes. The buildings are arranged around an open external space and an internal atrium that connects all of the building's wings.

The insertion is respectful to its surroundings and offers a minimalistic but elegantly gridded façade appearance, wrapping around classrooms, library, atrium and courtyards. The campus expresses a civic presence and openness and the architects (Reiach and Hall Architects and Michael Laird Architects) note that the project has created a 'truly public complex for a university that wants to have a presence in the city centre'. A retail edge along Cathedral Street adds commercial facilities that enhance both the life of the city and the experience of students. In addition, transparent ground floors allow for greater visibility of teaching and research activities and combined with physical permeability, the new circulation routes include quiet informal spaces between buildings for informal meetings and learning. The buildings previously occupied by the college are not left empty, but will be turned into a hotel and student accommodation.

All over the UK, educational institutions are redesigning their campuses to be more open to their surrounding communities, and invite the public into their buildings, spaces and cafes. This expresses universities' aspirations beyond the purely pragmatic, to be a catalyst for a better city. This relates to Strategy 9: Development of a vibrant university quarter.

Figs. 6.65–6.69 Glasgow's new City Campus regenerates an entire block in the city

Figs. 6.65–6.69   (continued)

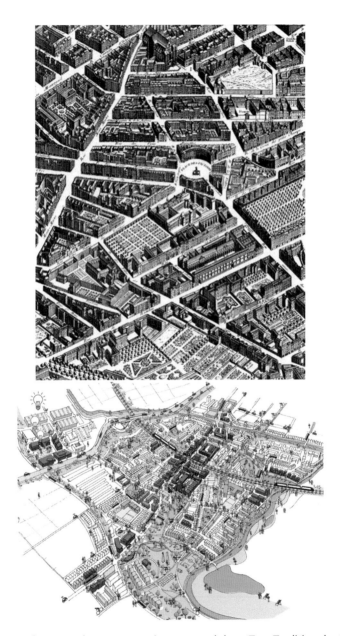

Figs. 6.70 and 6.71   Urban regeneration now and then. Top: Traditional urbanism is compact, mixed-use and walkable; most of traditional urbanism is sustainable urbanism—so regenerating the existing city and integrating historical buildings is a good way to make our cities more liveable, resource-efficient and resilient. Bottom: Innovation Hive for the Cambridge-to-Oxford Growth Corridor, town densification by Barton Willmore, 2017

Epilogue

Over the last 20 years, the introduction of a new model of urbanisation—which doesn't depend on expanding the city's footprint, but on consolidating and intensifying the existing city—has caused a paradigm shift in thinking for planners and architects. A paradigm shift is a sudden change that transforms domains and mind-sets. Previously it was always thought that urban planning theory proceeded slowly in logical steps, based on prior knowledge and tradition, rather than radical reform.

As this small book on urban regeneration has shown, there is a need for more knowledge and evidence on how to best deliver urban regeneration projects and how to avoid the pitfalls of projects that do not perform at the right level. Mistakes have been made in previous regeneration projects that have not been sufficiently mixed-use, ignored public transport, have only served a small 'luxury living' segment and triggered excessive gentrification.

Gentrification has emerged as a serious threat to socially just development.

Too many 'up-and-coming' areas in UK cities have ended up gentrified in a short time, became sanitised, were no longer creative and limited to the 'luxury living' segment—with devastating consequences for older residents and other vulnerable

© The Author(s) 2019
S. Lehmann, *Urban Regeneration*, https://doi.org/10.1007/978-3-030-04711-5

groups suffering disproportionate rent rise and social injustice—just think of some of the 'success story' neighbourhoods such as in Bristol's cultural quarter Stokes Croft, Manchester's bohemian Ancoats neighbourhood, Sheffield's Kelham Island, or Brighton's hip North Laines quarter (just to name a few). Like so many creative hubs before, they have become a victim of their own trendiness, and uncontrolled regeneration and rejuvenation projects have been the trigger for the twisted logic of gentrification processes.

Resisting gentrification, city councils need to understand these processes and put community-led measures in place to empower tenants against rising rents.

Gentrification is not inevitable! Working with the already existing community and older residents is a step towards avoiding gentrification. Local governments should keep good control of a project's delivery of social and environmental benefits to the existing surroundings. One of the benefits developers in Berlin have had regularly to commit to, is to build a minimum of 30 percent of new housing that is affordable and within the neighbourhood (not somewhere else), as well as commit to renting out cheap studio space to artists and various not-for-profit community organisations under market value. Artists contribute through their work to rising real estate value, and they are a community asset that any smart developer would like to keep in the quarter, as they achieve social good for the whole community as well as those who visit. City councils need to counteract gentrification and put effective regulations in place to limit the power of real estate owners, and to acknowledge and cooperate with those who regenerated the area in the first place.

My hope is that this 10-point strategy will work as an optimistic high-level guiding manifesto for decision makers in cities around the world. UK cities are a good example as they have a high level of liveability and relatively low carbon emissions, with plenty of lessons for others to aspire to. In the process of city transformation, I expect the following to become more relevant:

- New forms of systems thinking, co-operation and sharing are emerging.
- There are now tremendous opportunities for citizen-centric big data, but data sets are still fragmented, disconnected.
- We need integrated reliable city data that supports better urban governance, decision-making and leads to resource efficiency.
- All policies for cities should primarily be about health and public space improvement, reconnecting us with nature.
- There is a focus on residents' well-being and happiness, eg. improving long-term liveability for citizens, avoiding gentrification and isolation.

- We have seen a shift in scale from individual buildings to the urban design of building clusters, with retrofitting of existing neighbourhoods and better models for urban infill and densification.
- Apartment living will become much more common, with roof gardens and large balconies as outdoor space.
- The most successful regeneration projects are often modest and carefully inserted, rather than 'iconic vanity projects'.
- High-level guiding strategies as principles of good urbanism are necessary. This manifesto contributes towards this aim.
- Urban regeneration needs to be a people-led (rather than technology-led) process. In future, local people will be given a much bigger say over the sort of development to be built in their neighbourhood.
- Effective regulations have to be developed to counteract the threat of gentrification.

Cities are never finished objects, but always undergoing transformation. They are enormous real-world laboratories—they provide numerous examples of trial and error, of failures and successes. Nevertheless, their evolution and growth is always within an urban context, never isolated. The great Spanish architect Rafael Moneo noted (in an interview in 2017): 'I always resisted seeing a building as an isolated object. Everything I have done tries to relate the design to a broader social or urban context. Buildings are not the product of working in isolation but a co-dependent relationship with the city itself.'

The core strengths of our discipline are impact and innovation. This manifesto will go a long way towards supporting the urban transformation process. Its ten optimistic high-level guiding strategies are 'principles of good urbanism' that I hope will guide the urban regeneration of post-industrial cities worldwide. Their implementation is critical for a confident urban future, to advocate a new culture of urbanism and to crystallise what it means for UK cities to regenerate.

To this aim, the *Cluster for Sustainable Cities* has partnered with a number of key regional cities in the UK (including Brighton & Hove, Southend-on-Sea, Winchester) to collaborate with the business community and local governments to reshape these cities to become more innovative and dynamic. We hope to embrace opportunities for UK cities to reinvent themselves as highly liveable and resilient places. Together, we will carefully consider what action can be taken to regenerate the health of our UK cities and transform them into worthwhile habitable spaces. Please join us on this journey.

London and Las Vegas, December 2018   *Steffen Lehmann*

Further Reading on Urban Regeneration

'Urban Regeneration in the UK: Boom, Bust and Recovery', by James Evans and Phil Jones (Sage, 2008/2nd edn 2013).

'After Urban Regeneration: Communities, Policies and Place', edited by Dave O'Brien (Connected Communities, 2015).

'Innovations in Collaborative Urban Regeneration', edited by M. Horita and H. Koizumi (cSUR-UT Series, 2009).

'Urban Regeneration', by Ian Colquhoun (Batsford Publisher, 2016).

'Urban Regeneration in the UK', by Andrew Tallon (Routledge, 2013, 2nd edn).

'Shaping Change. 25 years of Urban Regeneration', by Julian Stock (2015).

'Urban Regeneration: A Handbook', edited by Peter Roberts, Hugh Skyes and Rachael Granger (British Urban Regeneration Association, 1999).

'Culture-led Urban Regeneration', edited by Ronan Paddison (Routledge, 2009).

'Smart Urban Regeneration: Visions, Institutions and Mechanisms for Real Estate', edited by Simon Huston (Routledge, 2017).

© The Author(s) 2019
S. Lehmann, *Urban Regeneration*, https://doi.org/10.1007/978-3-030-04711-5

'Bristol Is Open' research network platform for big data, see: https://www.
bristolisopen.com/

'Low Carbon Cities. Transforming Urban Systems', edited by Steffen Lehmann
(Earthscan from Routledge, 2015).

In the UK, useful guidance is provided by a number of organisations, including
the Commission for Architecture and the Built Environment (CABE), the Royal
Institute of British Architects (RIBA), the Academy of Urbanism (AoU), and the
Construction Industry Research and Information Association (CIRIA).

Prior to the production of this book, the *Urban Regeneration Manifesto* was presented by the author for feedback at a range of public events, including:

- Event series 'The Urban Future of Portsmouth' (2016–18)
- Bocconi University, Milano (Jan. 2018)
- University of Nevada, Las Vegas (Feb. 2018)
- University of Portsmouth (March 2018)
- University of Southern California, Los Angeles (March 2018)
- City of Helsinki, Finland (April 2018)
- Southend-on-Sea, UK (April 2018)
- Nicosia, Northern Cyprus (May 2018)
- Royal Society, CIRIA Annual Debate, London (June 2018)
- Xi'an Jiaotong University (June 2018)
- City of Brighton & Hove (July 2018)

The author can be contacted at the following email:
Steffen.Lehmann.Cities@gmail.com

© The Author(s) 2019
S. Lehmann, *Urban Regeneration*, https://doi.org/10.1007/978-3-030-04711-5

This book is proudly supported and endorsed by:

- The Academy of Urbanism (UK)
- ARUP
- The University of Nevada, Las Vegas (USA)
- The Cluster for Sustainable Cities (UK)
- CRUNCH - The Food-Water-Energy Nexus (EU)

CLUSTER FOR
SUSTAINABLE
CITIES

THE ACADEMY
OF URBANISM

ARUP

CRUNCH
The Food-Water-Energy Nexus

UNLV

 This project has received funding from the European Union's Horizon 2020 research and innovation programme under grant agreement No 730254.

Index

© The Author(s) 2019
S. Lehmann, *Urban Regeneration*, https://doi.org/10.1007/978-3-030-04711-5

Printed in Great Britain
by Amazon